I welcome this new study of the book of Job by Bill Long and Glandion Carney. These writers have a warm and personal approach to the book, and they show how Job's questions and search have not changed through the centuries. Glandion and Bill understand people, and that generous understanding of our struggles adds a powerful underscoring of Job's journey with God that we can draw upon to our own spiritual benefit.

EARL F. PALMER
pastor, University Presbyterian Church, Seattle

At last, a book on human brokenness, pain and suffering that
☐ is biblically and theologically rooted
☐ dares to ask the hard questions about where God is when we need him
☐ avoids all the clichés that offend rather than help those
who are in real pain.
This is a book I would feel comfortable giving to someone who is in the midst of tragedy, and who would resist anything that does not engage them at the level of their pain.

WALT GERBER
senior pastor, Menlo Park Presbyterian Church

A creative interweaving of reflections on poignant examples of present-day suffering with reflections on the book of Job, each illuminating the other. The authors follow the example of Job in never shrinking from honesty while never parting from faith. They don't conceal the fact that suffering endangers trust; neither do they lay guilt on the sufferer. They simply ask how trust can be recovered. It's that honest fidelity of their discussion that will help readers to recover their trust in God, even though not all their questions are answered.

NICHOLAS WOLTERSTORFF
Noah Porter Professor of Philosophical Theology, Yale Divinity School

This book presents Job as our instructor, challenger and encourager. The authors weave exegesis and example into a persuasive portrayal of the God who confirms Job's honesty and denounces the easy, "theologically correct" platitudes of well-meaning but shallow "comforters." One of the stories told is of a woman who was a victim of incest in her strict Christian home. Like Job, she has reached the spiritual maturity of "not feeling *bad* about not being sure whether God is *good*." God's truth, unlike some popular Christian clichés, really fits "the tangled web of life's complexity." *Trusting God Again* is a wise, clear-eyed, engaging and hopeful book.

PATRICK HENRY
executive director, Institute for Ecumenical and Cultural Research

WITHDRAWN

Regaining
Hope After
Disappointment
or Loss

Trusting GOD AGAIN

Glandion Carney
& William Long

Illustrations by Julie Bosacker

InterVarsity Press
Downers Grove, Illinois

128774

InterVarsity Press® is the book-publishing division of InterVarsity Christian Fellowship®, a student movement active on campus at hundreds of universities, colleges and schools of nursing in the United States of America, and a member movement of the International Fellowship of Evangelical Students. For information about local and regional activities, write Public Relations Dept., InterVarsity Christian Fellowship, 6400 Schroeder Rd., P.O. Box 7895, Madison, WI 53707-7895.

Cover photograph: Larry Williams/Masterfile

ISBN 0-8308-1609-7

Printed in the United States of America ∞

Library of Congress Cataloging-in-Publication Data

Carney, Glandion.
    Trusting God again: regaining hope after disappointment or loss/
Glandion Carney and William Long.
      p.   cm.
    ISBN 0-8308-1609-7
    1. Trust in God—Christianity.   2. Suffering—Religious aspects—
Christianity.   3. Spiritual healing.   4. Hope—Religious aspects—
Christianity.   5. Christian life.   6. Bible. O.T. Job—Criticism,
interpretation, etc.   I. Long, William Rudolf, 1952-
II. Title.
BV4637.C345   1995
248.8'6—dc20   95-7840
                                               CIP

15	14	13	12	11	10	9	8	7	6	5	4	3	2	1
07	06	05	04	03	02	01	00	99	98	97	96	95		

To our children,

who have brought us moments
of joy and endless surprises,
and who are our greatest encouragement
to trust God again:

Sydney Steele-Long, *vibrant*
Will Steele-Long, *focused*
Tia Lynn Carney, *wanderer*
Alyssa Carney, *controller*
Joy Carney, *direct*
Christopher Carney, *courageous*
Annie Carney, *happy*

INTRODUCTION

HOPING
TO TRUST

W e write this book for those who have been hurt, have suffered and wept and who still want to keep a vital faith and trust in the living God. We write to people acquainted with grief. Through this book, we hope to bring wisdom, consolation and guidance to you by studying the person of Job, who, like Jesus Christ, was a man of sorrows and acquainted with grief.

Growing up and getting older often seems to be as much a process of *loss* as of *growth*, though we are still unprepared for and saddened by the disappointment and distress which enter our lives. We build apparently secure fortresses against the distresses of life in several ways. We seek financial and physical security. We try to live healthy lives. We strive to internalize and practice all the right concepts that modern psychology and educational theory teach us—concepts such as respecting others, working cooperatively with them, not manipulating people around us, trying only to recognize the best in others, affirming *three* times before we criticize, attempting to maintain a positive attitude, and even smiling when it hurts. But when all is said and done, we simply cannot hide the fact that distress enters our seemingly impregnable forts with regularity and gnaws at us like the proverbial dog on the bone, or like the eagle on Prometheus's liver.

Distress discovers us in the varied situations of life. Sometimes it hits us like an exploding tidal wave; other times it seeps into our souls like a slow poison. Sometimes we think that distress is the last word we will ever hear in life. Like the psalmist, we say in dismay that all people are a vain hope (Psalm 116:11). Like the disciples on the Emmaus road, before they recognized Jesus in their midst, we tell people around us that we "had hoped that he was the one who was going to redeem" us (Luke 24:21). We had hoped that things would never turn out this badly. We had hoped that we would be spared some of the exquisite torment of life. Sometimes we lose an awareness of the present tense and the future tense in life.

Our goal in this book is to help you to discover the hopefulness of the present and the promise of the future. Yet we are under no illusions about the difficulty of our task. We live in a time where each new day discloses new torments for people. As I, Bill, write this, we are witnessing the greatest humanitarian disaster in a generation, the virtual destruction of the people of Rwanda. Distress also strikes at a more personal level. Two Christian friends are on my mind now, friends on whom distress has descended like a sudden tornado, friends who have no time for pious platitudes and easy answers, but who want to maintain faith and trust in a loving God.

Meet Ann, a woman in her forties, a lifelong friend of my wife. Ann has always been a positive, outgoing, dedicated Christian woman. When she and her husband, Robert, had children, they decided that despite the financial hardship it would entail, Ann would stay home and provide a healthy and supportive environment for their two daughters. She threw herself into motherhood with a commitment and verve second to none.

Then life changed suddenly. During a routine gynecological exam, Ann discovered that she had an advanced form of ovarian cancer. The great irony is that Ann always has taken scrupulous care of herself. She ate the best foods, exercised regularly and did everything she could to maintain physical and spiritual health. Ann underwent immediate surgery and extensive chemotherapy and, at this writing, will soon be moving to Seattle to undergo a new cancer treatment at the Fred Hutchinson Clinic. Ann and Robert try to remain upbeat in all this, but this fiery trial has rushed through their lives like a windblown prairie grass fire.

Robert now has to spend nearly all of his time working or being with Ann. Ann can only see the children a few hours a day. Friends from the church and elsewhere have lent a helping hand, but the stress is obvious. One morning their eight-year-old, Megan, came to Ann's bedside and burst into tears. "Mommy," she said, "I hate this disease. It takes you away from me and now it takes daddy away too." This is their life today.

A second friend, Tim, is experiencing distress of another sort. Tim is one of my jogging partners, a handsome, outgoing, athletic businessman in his late thirties with all the outward signs of success in life. Yet he and his wife have come to such a devastating impasse in their marriage that a divorce seems imminent. The wounds are fresh and deep. Every attempt at conversation only breeds another explosion. Counselors and pastors have tried unsuccessfully to resolve the issues between them. Now the only professionals they deal with are the attorneys. The impending divorce is tearing up Tim. He has to begin life again even while he is thinking that he would do anything to have aspects of the old life back. He sleeps fitfully; he is no longer in his own bed. He has the feeling that things will get worse before they get better. A second optimistic friend has been plunged into gloom—a gloom that envelops an entire family unit.

These are the real distresses of life that we, for all of our vaunted scientific achievements and psychological awareness, cannot escape. We cannot wish them away. A course in positive thinking or tapes by motivational speakers might yield some positive results, but the reality of their lives and, often, ours is that we have been bludgeoned *by* life.

Distress is like an insistent landlord that must be paid, like a representative from the collection agency who simply will not leave until an agreement for repayment is made. Distress is like Shylock in Shakespeare's

Merchant of Venice, who will exact his pound of flesh out of the choicest part of us simply because it is owed. Distress is not something that we can just dismiss.

Our Purpose
Our major purpose in this book is to give you encouragement and clear biblical guidance on how to maintain a vital and vibrant trust in God as you experience and move through your distress. Though the waves of distress often threaten to sink or capsize us, we believe, as the book of Job teaches, that God is a strong anchor for us, an anchor in whom we must continue to trust, and an anchor which holds us firm, offering life and hope. We will find, as Jonah did in the belly of the whale, that God listens to us in our deepest distress; God hears us even when we are dragging along the depths of the ocean floor. God hears us because, in the beautiful words of the church father Augustine, "the ears of God are in the heart of the one who calls."

The purpose of this book is to help you regain and maintain a vibrant, dynamic and confident trust in God in the midst of your sadness. The psalmist says, "You prepare a table before me *in the presence* of my enemies" (Psalm 23:5). Yes. Right in the middle of pain, anxiety, uncertainty and threatening death, God is there working for your benefit. Often the traces of God's activity can only be perceived as in a glass dimly, but they are there. We would like to show you how to perceive the traces of God's loving care in your daily life.

To help us in this task, we will be studying the book of Job together. Job was a person of faith who experienced the suddenness of dramatic loss. He felt his loss deeply and clung to his pain and his God in eloquent, passionate and persistent speeches. Finally, he received a surprising but life-changing response from God. Job is able to help us, who face distresses not unlike his, to feel our pain, articulate our thoughts, persist in our complaint, keep approaching God and, finally, to have the grace to recognize and see God in a new way through our pain. Job will be a wise conversation partner and guide for us who face the same difficult issues of trusting God with our present and future.

In addition to Job, we would also like you to meet some of our friends. To understand the book of Job, we think that we need to filter his words through the felt experience of people in our day. We would like to introduce you to Deb and Barry, a Christian couple in their forties who have had to deal in the last year with the rupture of Deb's silicone breast implants, implants she received in 1976 after a battle with breast cancer. She received the implants then in order "to make her whole"; now the seepage threatens her life.

We would like you to meet Tedd and Julie, a couple in their thirties, who faced the sudden death of their two-year-old son, Will, on April 10, 1993, as a result of a farm accident. We would like to introduce you to Sheri, a woman in her late thirties, a mother of four, married to David, who has been struck afresh by the powerful memories of childhood sexual abuse which she experienced over several years from her father, who was a minister, and from two brothers. We want you to meet Ron, an eleven-year-old boy infected with the HIV virus, which he inherited from his parents. Ron is struggling with issues of fairness and trust in God and in people.

We introduce you to these and others not principally to evoke sympathy for them. In most cases they have their circles of friends who provide as much comfort as can be expected. We introduce them, with their permission, because they are trying to live faithful Christian lives in the midst of these losses. Sometimes they "win"; but sometimes they feel overwhelmed like the psalmist, when he says, "all your waves and breakers have swept over me" (Psalm 42:7). In the final analysis we tell their stories alongside the story of Job because we feel that if Christian faith and the Scriptures are to be vital today, they must be so for those who have *suffered most dramatically* and experienced most grievous losses, as well as for those of us whose losses have not been so all-consuming. Let us listen to the conversation between Job and his friends and Job and our friends and find *ourselves* anew as we seek to trust God for the present and the future.

How to Use This Book

This book is a conversation of sorts—a conversation among Job, his and our friends and you, the reader. It is part of that great conversation, old as the world and deep as the sea, about living and loving and suffering and trusting God. We hope that in the following pages you will feel free to join in the conversation with Job, us and the friends.

We have written this book for individual and group study. Each chapter is written so that you might understand your life and Job's experience better. Part one sets the tone and defines the issue of our book: the problem of trust and loss. Chapter one describes the importance of trust for life, the breaking of trust and the remaking of trust. Chapters two and three tell the story of Job's loss in detail, as well as his reaction to it.

Part two explores in detail Job's and our various losses, with special attention to how we react to these losses. For example, in view of his loss, Job is full of anger and grief at his friends and God. So we take up the themes of anger, grief and friends in chapters four through six, and we show how each played a major role for Job as well as for us.

Part three consists of chapters seven through ten and is concerned with the complexities of restored trust and the pain and difficulty of regaining hope after great distress. The questions that interest us in these chapters are, How do we turn the corner from grief to trust again? Is trust restored quickly or slowly? What specific practices did Job do, and what can we do, to regain our trust? And, finally, is it really possible to be restored after we have been shattered? Job helps us frame the questions and suggest some surprising but helpful answers.

In several of the chapters we tell our friends' stories, and in every chapter we discuss the text of Job in detail. We try to give you all the sections of Job that you will need to understand this book. As we conclude each chapter, we provide a prayer and a series of discussion questions. The purpose of the prayer is to help you bring together the themes and ideas of the chapter in one statement, which you can speak back to God. We provide questions so that you may take the time to probe your own life and to personalize the book of Job.

Finally, the conclusion of this book is designed to summarize, draw out and apply the results of our study for personal discipleship. We will have succeeded in our task if you recommit yourself to the life of faith, whether you are in distress or not. If you, like Job, see God in a new and fresh way through this book, we will be more than gratified.

A Personal Word

This is the second book we have written together. The first, *Longing for God: Prayer and the Rhythms of Life* (InterVarsity, 1993), is an exposition of thirty psalms, under the headings of Longing, Distress, Trust and Praise. In that book we described our working method and gave a word about how the book grew out of our personal experience.

We need only say a few things here. Though two people have contributed to this book, we most frequently use "I" in the following pages to refer to ourselves. The "I" does not mean that we have both experienced every story we tell; it means that we both embrace the truth of which the "I" speaks.

This book, as did *Longing for God*, has grown out of the tangle and simplicity of our own lives. I, Glandion, took a temporary pastoral assignment in 1993 after several years in executive positions in Christian organizations. In my interracial congregation in Minneapolis I discovered in a fresh way the daily battering and beatings to which many people are subject, abuses that I certainly had witnessed but was somewhat removed from in my executive positions. I saw, above all, that people in distress today need a friend. They need someone to talk to—someone who is acquainted with their grief and can bear their sorrow. Job, the patient and not-so-patient sufferer was the one to whom I naturally turned, because he was a sufferer who experienced significant loss but never stopped trusting God.

I, Bill, began my serious study of the book of Job in 1990 after being asked by a senior citizens' group to lead a Lenten Bible study in Portland, Oregon. I chose Job at the time for a reason that is becoming clearer to me all the time—for a considerable period between 1986 and 1993 I was in distress. When I taught Job in 1990, it was as if I *became* Job. I could read my own distress in and out of Job, and I could earnestly teach the issues of Job's life because, in fact, they were issues of my life. After Glandion and I finished our book on the Psalms, it seemed appropriate to take up the issue of trusting God again. Trust is an issue for both of us and, we believe, is an issue for many people today.

We devoted an entire section of *Longing for God* to trust. For so many people, and you may be one, trust, which is so necessary for life, has been shattered. Can trust be restored? How? Is learning to trust God again related to restoring our trust in people? Can I really say that I trust God if I have a hard time trusting people? *Must* I try again to trust people who have hurt me in order to claim that I am really trusting God again?

Our prayer is that the following thoughts may help you explore your own hurts, your attitude toward others and toward God, and that through this you may be led to trust God again for the present and the future.

Last, but certainly not least, we would like to extend our sincere gratitude and appreciation to Julie Bosacker for the moving drawings in this book. Julie's work captures the glory, intensity and pain of Job. May her drawings touch your heart, as they have touched ours.

PART 1

THE PROBLEM
OF TRUST
& LOSS

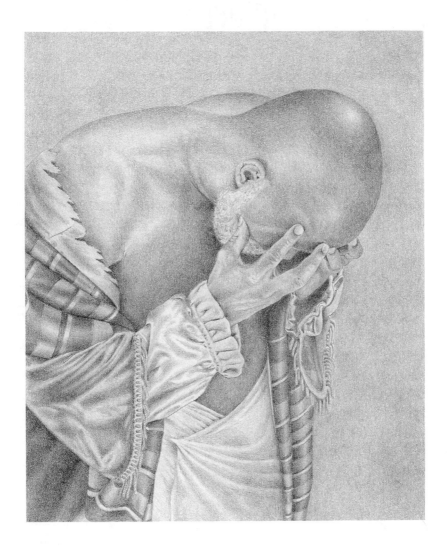

JOB 1:20-21
At this, Job got up and tore his robe and shaved his head. Then he fell to the ground in worship
and said:
"Naked I came from my mother's womb,
And naked I will depart.
The LORD gave and the LORD has taken away;
may the name of the LORD be praised."

1

TRUST:
THE ELIXIR
OF LIFE

Ron is an eleven-year-old boy whom I, Glandion, met through a mutual friend. I first met Ron when he was in the hospital, where he was admitted because of a 105-degree fever. I learned that his parents were both carriers of the HIV virus, that his mother had died of AIDS the previous year, that his father was an alcoholic and that Ron also was HIV-positive.

Before I entered his hospital room, I had a silent discussion with myself. *What do I have to say to this boy?* I thought. *What can I possibly offer him? Should I try to give him consolation? Hope? Anything? How can I possibly hear what Ron has to say?* For a desperate moment I wondered if I should even be there. I said a prayer, almost as much for myself as for Ron. Then I entered his room.

Ron lay on the bed before me. He was listless and withdrawn. The fever had sapped his strength, and I began to recognize the way this horrible disease works: it gradually sucks the energy, verve and life out of even its youngest victims. It is what doctors call an "opportunistic" disease—it finds an "opportunity" through another weakness, and then it attacks with all its fury. I greeted Ron, and he reluctantly returned my greeting. I asked him how he was feeling. He said that he didn't know.

At that moment I didn't know how I felt. So I tried another tack. "Ron," I said, "do you feel *inward?*"

"What does *inward* mean?" he responded. There was a brief flicker of life and interest.

"When you feel inward you have all of your feelings inside you," I said. "You may be angry and frightened and anxious, but all of your feelings are jumbled together and none wants to come out. Sometimes you feel happy, sometimes sad, but you can't really say what you feel. Is that it, Ron?"

"That's it," he responded quietly. "I feel inward." He turned away.

That was the extent of our first conversation. I knew, however, that I had been able to breach Ron's trust barrier and enter his heart. This was confirmed for me as I was on my way out of the room. The nurse had just entered. With a big smile she asked Ron, "Ron, how do you feel today?"

Ron responded, "I feel inward." Ron and I chuckled while the nurse's smile was replaced by a look of confusion. We would talk again.

The next day I returned. Ron was feeling much better. The fever had left him. He was animated and alert. I had discovered from his friends that he loved to draw, and so I brought him crayons, pencils and a sketch pad. We didn't talk as much that day. I just asked him to draw what it meant to feel inward. He worked quietly and intently.

After a while I thought I would say a few words to him. "Ron, do you know what it means to trust God?" He didn't respond. This time I felt I understood his silence.

"It's like this," I said. I took off my wedding ring, opened my shirt pocket and dropped it in. "Trust is like that, Ron. It's like taking the thing that is dearest to you and dropping it right into your heart, just like a farmer would drop a seed into the ground. Then, as it touches your heart, it becomes warm and begins to grow. Trust is like that—to take the most precious thing that you have and drop it right into your heart. God is then the one who nurtures it and makes it warm and makes it grow."

This may not be the most brilliant story anyone has ever told about trust. But Ron liked it. He mentioned to me how much he liked it. When I saw him a few days later riding his bike and playing with his friends, we smiled and greeted each other. I began to see Ron's physical struggle as a picture of a deeper spiritual struggle which he, and many of us, endure all the time. Ron's struggle was not simply to get better physically, but also to trust the great *invisible* force in the universe, God, when other *visible* forces were not much comfort at all.

Thinking About Trust

Ron's story tugs at our hearts and makes us weep for all the tangled things in our relationships and our past that have led to destruction and pain. His story also stimulates us to think about trust, its meaning and importance for our lives. For most of this book I will, with the help of the book of Job, explore the complexities of lost and restored trust. At first, though, I need to establish a context in which to understand Job's and our losses. For the rest of this chapter I will reflect with you on the centrality of trust in establishing and maintaining human relationships and the fabric of Christian faith.

Etymologically, *trust* is related to the word *true,* and *true* in Middle English is probably derived from the word *tree.* A tree is true. That means that it is straight and firm. For a person to be true, or trustworthy, therefore, means that the person is straight and firmly rooted. Trust, then, is something that is deeply rooted, like the tree, and is something that is straight and "true," like the tree. Whenever I use the word *trust,* then, I think of something stable and firm that, like the tree, provides shade and protection. When I say, "I trust God," I mean that I exercise firm and stable confidence in God.

It is my experience that trusting others and God is essential to human happiness and spiritual well-being. Augustine claimed that God has made us for himself and that our hearts are restless until they find their rest in God. I maintain that we are made to trust, and that without trust our lives become deeply unsatisfying and empty. Without trust we have no friends and no closeness, no sense that we are connected in any vital way to people. We need to trust people in order to live, and we need to have a sense that the Ruler of the universe is trustworthy.

The instinct to trust is built into our genes and passed from generation to generation with as much certainty as skin color is passed on from parent to child. Observe young children. They will often perform acts involving great physical danger because they are told to do so by someone they trust. When parents trust children or lovers trust each other, they become open to tremendously intimate and powerful acts of communication and love. Trust means that we are truly committed to the growth and basic integrity of the other person. With trust, people flourish. How many times have we heard, when athletes are interviewed after a victory or when people have accomplished something significant, that the victors attribute a large part of their success to someone's believing in them? To believe in someone is to trust or to have confidence in them. Trust nurtures faith in the other and expects the best from another person. In 1 Corinthians 13 Paul says that love "always protects, always trusts, always hopes, always perseveres" (v. 7). A trusting person is one who has learned how to love.

Breaking Trust

Yet trust is very fragile, as fragile and brittle as a clay pot in bone-dry state. Trust is like an exotic and sensitive flowering plant that flourishes only under optimal conditions but tends to fade, wither and die when struck by severe adversity. So trust can quickly, powerfully and sometimes irretrievably be broken. Behind every shattered life and every strained relationship is a story of broken trust, of "truth" that went astray, of a "tree" that is no longer deeply rooted.

We grow up with a tightly bound web of trust-expectations that have been shaped in us from our birth and sometimes from before our birth. No spider's web, however intricately designed and flawlessly executed, is half as complex as the simplest person's web of trust relationships and beliefs. Many of our trust-expectations are so intimate and personal that when they are broken, we feel personally attacked and humiliated.

Trust may be broken between individuals and groups, but more subtly and powerfully, trust can be broken between individuals and God. The breaking of trust between individuals is captured in the following phrases: "But *you* led me to believe that," or "That was definitely *not* part of the agreement," or "You didn't say *that*." Sometimes the violations of our trust are relatively minor and can be patched up in conversation and through getting to know the other person better.

At times, however, no words are powerful enough to capture the debilitating experience of broken trust. Words like *treachery, betrayal, disloyalty* or *fraud* are often too frail to bear the heavy weight of broken trust. In his classic work, *The Inferno*, Dante reserves the lowest level of hell for those who break relationships where trust ought to be assured. To this hell of hells Dante consigns those who have broken trust with their benefactors, such as Judas, who betrayed Christ, the author of life. The breaking of trust, like no other experience, tends to reduce us to the bare essentials of our nature. We've been attacked and we're hurt, but in addition we feel exposed and ridiculed. We feel that our privacy and our vulnerability have been hung out on the line for every passerby to gawk at. Often, as a result we explode in anger, rage and desire for vengeance.

We not only experience private acts of betrayal or breaking of trust. We are living in a society where increasingly we are bearing the costs of broken trust. We spend billions of dollars yearly on therapists and attorneys and other professionals to help us regain our financial and spiritual dignity when trust has been broken. But beyond the considerable financial costs, there are the subtle and not-so-subtle psychological costs of the breaking of trust in our society. Three examples will illustrate this.

The first shows how broken trust adds to racial problems in our country. When I speak with young people about their fears and hopes, they say that one of their greatest fears is personal safety, and one of the biggest threats to personal safety is the widespread existence of gangs. Having talked to a number of young people about gangs, I've concluded that by a "gang" they mean any group of five or more youths of a different ethnic group from themselves, who are gathered together in a public place. Yet when I ask if they ever get together in groups of five or more, they respond, "Oh sure, I always hang around with my friends."

Gang is the latest word in American English that permits and even encourages negative stereotyping of ethnic and racial groups. Trust is broken between our young people of different races and ethnic groups before a name is known or a problem understood.

The second and third examples involve relationships between men and women in our culture. With the heightened awareness of sexual harassment in our society, an awareness that has brought about a number of positive changes in the work place, comes the following realities. Sam, a professor friend of mine in his late forties, confessed to me that he no longer asks about students' personal lives, for fear that they might interpret this as the teacher's attempt to subtly seduce them and then, in response, slap a sexual harassment grievance or lawsuit on him. Sam said that ten years ago, when he taught in a high school, he would often, as a way of bolstering a girl's self-image, mention how attractive she looked or how he appreciated her care for herself. Now, he says, "I would rather have a job and sacrifice my personal interactions with students than perhaps endanger my career by being thought to have crossed someone else's mental line."

This issue cuts both ways as the following example from Lynn, a pastor, shows. Lynn mentioned to me that she no longer hugs her male parishioners for fear that someone may feel that she is giving signals that exceed her intention. Lynn says that issues of sexuality, which she had always seen as "fun and challenging," were now simply too dangerous to have anything to do with. Again, for Lynn, it is better to hold back and perhaps miss a special moment of grace with a person than to risk opening herself to someone else's unpredictable behavior, possible condemnation by church and society, and the distinct probability of not being able to get another pastoral position.

Finally, the male-female relationship in our culture brings other kinds of suspicion and mistrust. Tom tells how he, a married man, has developed a friendship with a married woman. They like to eat lunch together occasionally and keep up with each other's lives and family. But they are discovering that society doesn't permit them to do this openly. Questions, stares and suggestive comments from friends and others who know them make them wonder if it is possible in our society to have a friend of the opposite sex openly or whether one has to be driven to secret meetings, clandestine trysts and the desire to hide what one is doing so that no one finds out.

We all agree that boundaries need to be established in human relationships as in almost everything else. Boundaries keep us from hurting and getting hurt and, to a lesser or greater extent, give us a "playground" in which to explore and discover the world. But our litigious society, our suspicious society, our society which does not trust its own members, is increasingly drawing the boundaries around us very narrowly. The not-so-subtle message of our society to its members is that life is a jungle, that others are probably trying to hurt you, that you will probably regret it if you extend yourself to others and that it is safest and healthiest to stay with your own kind in like-minded communities and pray every night that nothing terrible happens to your loved ones.

The breaking of trust exacts a gargantuan toll from us. Often the toll is invisible, like the building up of instability under a mound of earth that is fed by an underground stream, until the final breaking point comes. Then we feel deeply, in the core of our being, that we have become disconnected from other people and disoriented in an increasingly complex world. The breaking of trust may affect our physical health. It certainly affects the way we relate to people. We begin to feel more tentative, we reach out less often to other people, we expect less from each successive human encounter, and we tumble into our own form of isolation. When we lose trust, we feel that we have lost our moorings, our coordination and our spiritual equilibrium. We fall back into fear, and live with paranoia.

For, fundamentally, the breaking of trust means that the rules we thought applied to us and to others really do not apply. We *thought* that if we loved our children and took care of them, everything *ought* to work out well with them. They *should* grow up happy and healthy. But often it is not so. We *thought* that if we took care of ourselves, ate the right foods and exercised properly, we *should not* have to face sudden, premature and perhaps fatal diseases of the body. We *thought* that if we applied ourself to the job and worked well and loyally, we *ought* to get rewarded by security, promotion, greater respect and higher compensation. We *thought* that if we tried to be faithful and loving and affirming of a spouse, they *ought* to respond to us in kind and be grateful for all the care we lavished on them. We *thought* that if we were willing to extend ourselves to help someone else, they would not use our help to hurt us in some way.

We know that life comes neither with an owner's manual nor with money-back guarantees. But we have been brought up as intense believers in rules, rules that we believe ought to assure our happiness and promote harmony in society. When the rules seem to be so utterly violated, we scream for vengeance and compensation, and we wonder if anything is assured in this fleeting mortal life.

Breaking Trust with God

Finally, the breaking of trust affects not simply us and our loved ones or us and a group of people; it also affects us *and God*. Though many deny it, the misery in our lives is often a result of broken trust between us and God. Just as we have expectations of our family, friends and work, so we have expectations of God. One of the reasons we expect so much from God is that he promises so much in his Word. For years when my path was not straight I would daily recite Proverbs 3:5-6 to God:

Trust in the LORD with all your heart
　　and lean not on your own understanding;
in all your ways acknowledge him,
　　and he will make your paths straight.

I understate the case. I would not recite these words to God; I would shove them in God's face. I would shout the verses in my room and say,

"Don't you see this word, God? Don't you agree this is your word? Aren't you promising a straight path to the one who trusts you fully? Don't you know that I, though I am a sinner, am trying to trust you with my life?"

I became angry, estranged and alienated from God. I felt that God was not being true to his word, and it caused me intense agony. It made me question for several years whether God really was good. Intellectually I knew that the Scripture taught that God is good and that the steadfast love of the Lord endures forever, but I was feeling let down in the core of my being, and that feeling of abandonment or betrayal made my life spin more and more out of control.

Examine your life. Do you ever feel that God is really the one responsible for your misery? I believe that most of us feel that we may have contributed something to our predicament but that it is, in fact, God who really needs to explain himself for our misfortune. Unless you have a sense that God may have betrayed you, or unless you have an appreciation of how some Christians may feel this way, you will not be able to understand or appreciate the book of Job.

The breaking of trust shatters lives. Confident people can be transformed overnight into shattered hulks of tormented humanity. The sure step becomes tentative; the genial and outgoing person becomes withdrawn and withered. Is there a remedy for broken trust? Is there a way to rebuild a shattered life? Is it possible to trust God again?

Remaking Trust

In one of the most moving and beautiful chapters of biblical poetry Job asks, "If a man dies, will he live again?" (Job 14:14). We need only to change Job's question slightly for our own purposes: If a person loses trust, can that person trust again? If trust is broken, can it be restored? If you have been devastated by an act which violated you deeply, can you learn to trust life and people and God again? Or must you forever alternately nurse or treasure your hurt, believing that your injury is so unique and so powerful that it's beyond healing?

Two stories, one apparently trite and one definitely serious, will help focus the discussion. The first one is about a trip my son and I (Bill) made from Kansas to Denver (about four hundred miles) in 1993. He was six years old at the time and had just discovered the joy of collecting National Basketball Association sports cards. He loved the Michael Jordan and Charles Barkley cards that he got, but a special favorite for him on this trip was a Patrick Ewing card, which we purchased for six dollars. It was his most valuable card. So valuable was it for Will that he would not let it out of his hands. He carried it in the car; he slept with it next to him in bed; he brought it to the hotel restaurant for breakfast. Though the card was in a protective plastic envelope, it soon bent under the rough and unpredictable handling of an eager six-year-old. Of course, when he saw that the card was bent, he was crestfallen. The card, in Will's language, was "ruined." He cast it down in disgust, anger and sadness and vowed never to collect another card again. Only when I assured him that there were other card shops in the world beyond Denver, Colorado and Sterling, Kansas and that perhaps we could treat cards with more care in the future did he regain his composure. A little bit of trust was broken—and restored.

A more serious example comes from the riveting *New York Times Magazine* story of a woman, a professor of philosophy from a distinguished university, who had been raped while she was in Europe on sabbatical. The rape immediately became the most all-consuming and compelling experience in her life. She described her life as shattered, like a piece of expensive china suddenly dropped on a hard tile floor. She relived the experience again and again. She tried to figure out if there could have been a way to avoid it, and she thought about the various ways she would have liked to wreak vengeance on her attacker. Then she went on to tell of her gradual healing process as she, aided by a loving husband, friends and a counselor, vowed to see the rape and its aftermath as contributing to her greater strength rather than to her destruction.

The woman was certainly not an escapist. Yet she clearly saw that to keep from being repeatedly attacked by the rapist in her mind, she needed to visualize the shattered pieces coming together and held together by an adhesive stronger than even the hardest tessellated tile on which a plate could fall. In order to live again, to trust again, she had to see her life fused with unbreakable steel.

My purpose in this book is to show that trust *can* be restored and that you can be a stronger, deeper and more insightful person for having experienced your distress. I am *not* saying that the experience of rape or severe loss is good. I am also not saying that you need to work with or spend your life with the person who has broken trust with you just to prove that you have overcome your distress. I *am* claiming that an open, affirming and trusting attitude to life and God can be restored and a new receptivity and life-affirming insight into people can be developed through trusting God again. As a matter of fact, the person injured can, in faith, begin to see the injury or hurt as an asset in his or her spiritual inventory. Though you never would have chosen the hurt, if you had the choice, now that you have experienced the hurt you can see it as a special gift from God to you, a gift which can be used to strengthen and bring life to others. The fire that *burned you can now be a fire that warms* someone else.

I am convinced that God has equipped us with a powerful capacity to affirm life in the midst of death and to keep on believing in his healing power even in the most severe circumstances. This affirmation of life, or, in the words of the title, this trusting again, will not come as a result of denying or blocking out the hurt that came our way. I will try to show that restored trust happens as you first affirm your pain very deeply and then try to see this unexpected and shattering event as the first step on the new path of life that you have not chosen but that you now are privileged to walk. The apostle Paul, who himself knew great distress, states that his goal in life is "to know Christ and the power of his res-urrection and the fellowship of sharing in his sufferings" (Philippians 3:10). For Paul the way of suffering and distress united him to Christ and gave him an intimacy in relationship to Christ that nothing else could quite provide (the Greek word for fellowship is *koinonia*, the word Christians use to describe the unity of the body of Christ).

29

Three Steps in Recovering Our Trust

My major point in this book, to reiterate, is that trust in God and in life *can* be restored. It is not easy nor is it painless to do so, but it can happen. For the remainder of this chapter I will mention three ideas derived from the book of Job that I will develop throughout the book; all three are crucial to restoring this trust.

First, we need to honestly recount our experience of pain and our feelings about our experience. We need to tell our story to someone—maybe it is to God or to friends or to our diary. The point is not where or to whom you tell it; you need to tell it. Don't flinch. Don't sugarcoat the feelings. Tell the story over and over again until you can tell it *calmly.* Tell it in your own way. As we will see with Job, he hardly talks at all about how much the loss of his family and his wealth means to him; he spends more time exploring how he feels, what he wants of his friends and God, and why he feels that God has treated him unjustly. It is important to stress that we are not ready to trust God again until we can tell our story *calmly.* This is the first step to trusting God and others with your story. If you can tell your story fully and calmly, you show that it no longer has control over you. *You* now choose the words to explain it; *you* are the master of telling the story; you will not let the painful thing dominate you as it has done in the past.

Second, we need to never let go of God as we seek an explanation for our distress. This does *not* mean that we always appear meek and submissive before him. Never letting go of God means that we keep bringing our prayer and complaint to him in all its raw power and debilitating capacity. A beautiful biblical picture of never letting God go is in Genesis 32, where Jacob, left by himself at night, wrestled with his opponent—the angel of God—all night long. As dawn approached and the supernatural creature was about to withdraw, Jacob said, "I will not let you go unless you bless me" (Genesis 32:26). *That* is the attitude and posture Christians in distress need toward God: "I will not let you go, my God, until you make this bane into a blessing, until you make this prison into a palace, until you make this horrendous way into a blessed way."

Third, even as we hold on to God, we need to be ready to admit that we do not have the whole story or the whole truth. This crucial step is perhaps the most difficult one to take precisely because when we reflect deeply on and feel our pain, *we know that our pain is true;* that is, we know that our pain is as real to us as the beating of our heart. But in our distress, we begin to think that the *entire explanation for our distress is in our experience* of it. If someone comes in and gives an alternative explanation for our distress, we feel they are being glib and judgmental and that they do not understand us. Even though we may not want an alternative explanation as much as we want comfort in our distress, the fact remains that for healing to take place and for trust to be remade, we will need to change our thinking. We will, ultimately, have to give up our pain to God and receive back from God not simply the comfort that only he can give, but also a different understanding of our pain. We who have been saying "It hurts so badly!" may never be told *why* it hurts so much, but still we need to relinquish our demand for an explanation on our terms, and let God explain it in his own way. As the hymn says, "God is his own interpreter, and He will make it plain."

Prayer

Our sovereign God, give me courage to recognize my hurt, and give me eyes to see the hurt of others. Somehow I picked up the notion, dear God, that life should have been easier, that the distresses of life ought not to have hit me so strongly, that I would be exempt from the debilitating pains of living. But I have to say in all honesty that hurt has found me. Sometimes I don't know what to call the hurt, since when I cry in pain my words are not too logical. The ache is sometimes too general and too diffuse. But sometimes I feel as if I have been betrayed and let down, that trust has been broken, that I have been cast aside. I am in need of strength, but even more, Father, I feel a need for restoration, for rebuilding, for the freshness and newness that only you can bring. Restore my soul and help me thereby be an instrument to help others regain their strength. I pray in the name of Jesus Christ the Lord, amen.

Questions for Study and Discussion

1. Has your trust in someone ever been betrayed? What can you tell or write about it?

2. What words and feelings capture the reality of your loss of trust? Be as specific as you can.

3. Have you decided to trust God again, or are you unable to go beyond the feeling of betrayal and breaking of trust that you experienced?

4. If you are trying to trust him again and to lead a restored life, what are you doing differently? Is there more or less satisfaction in it?

5. What role do you think God plays in your learning to trust again?

A BRIEF REFLECTION ON A FAVORITE POEM

One of the most powerful poetic examinations of trust I know is Robert Frost's "The Road Not Taken." In this poem Frost is not explicitly speaking about how to trust again, but his focus on the meaning and effect of choices we make is perfectly attuned to the centrality of trust for faithful living. The first three stanzas are familiar to us:

Two roads diverged in a yellow wood,
And sorry I could not travel both
And be one traveler, long I stood
And looked down one as far as I could
To where it bent in the undergrowth;

Then took the other, as just as fair,
And having perhaps the better claim,

Because it was grassy and wanted wear . . .

Oh, I kept the first for another day!
Yet knowing how way leads on to way,
I doubted if I should ever come back.

Frost creates a powerful picture: he is walking through the woods and comes to a fork in the road. Both paths look about the same, but one, because it appears a bit less traveled, beckons him. As he goes on this path he thinks back on the other path—the road not taken—and says, "Oh, I kept the first for another day," probably because he believes there will be time to return and trace the other path. Yet because he knows "how way leads on to way," he says, "I doubted if I should ever come back."

Two roads, one choice. Frost's choice is not a forced situation, like many of our distresses. We simply would not, if given the choice, have selected them. But once Frost has made his decision, he finds that he never returns to the other path. Once we have encountered distress, we too walk down that path and do not return to the first path or the other way. Like Frost, we think wistfully about the first path and wonder what it must be like to be able to take that well-worn path, but it is simply not to be. Frost cannot retrace his steps, even though he would like to do so, because he knows "how way leads on to way." We cannot go back to the other path, because the horrors of our distress block the way. In both cases we are on one path and do not return to the other.

But what shall we say about this *new* path? And how do we remember the old path which we have either chosen to leave or been forced to leave? How can we say that this new path, whether forced or chosen, is really a *good* path, the *right* path for us? How can we say that the new path is the path in which God is alive and active and to be trusted? What if God was only on the *other* path, the path not chosen? The last stanza of Frost's poem leads us to an answer.

I shall be telling this with a sigh
Somewhere ages and ages hence:

Two roads diverged in a wood, and I—
I took the one less travelled by,
And that has made all the difference.

In the last stanza Frost tries to discover the meaning of the less traveled path. He cannot escape the constant thought that the other path, the one he didn't take, might have been better. He says, "I shall be telling this with a sigh." Why tell the story of your life with a sigh unless you believe that the other path might have been better? That the other school or the other job might have been better? That somehow that which is now closed to us really held the promise to the true joys of life? Why do waves of nostalgia flood over us when we relive our earlier days, unless we believe that somehow the great promise of those days should have turned out somewhat differently from the stark reality of these days?

In the first line of the last stanza it is almost as if Frost is wavering in his own uncertainty. But the final two lines, the most memorable, show his confidence.

I took the one less travelled by,
And that has made all the difference.

Frost's point is that even though other choices were available, his choice of the less traveled path was good and powerful and meaningful for him. It made all the difference for him.

In order to regain our spiritual health and be able to trust God again, we need to be able to say with Frost that the less traveled way (in our case, the way of distress) has made all the difference for us. We certainly would never have chosen the way of pain. To lose a child or a loved one, to suffer a debilitating illness or injury, to experience personal violation or to go through years of depression is not the choice of any sane person. But once we are placed on that new and strange path, we need to see how "way leads on to way." We need to see how the new and painful path has its own rhythm and contours and spiritual dynamics that are very different from those of the first path. When we recognize how "way leads on to way," in the new and painful path, we begin to catch its meaning, its promise and even its joy.

That is why the closing words of the poem, "And that has made all the difference," are really a profound statement of faith. They say that this new path, this strange path, is the path that gives us life. What we might at one time have seen as something that threatened to suck every ounce of vital energy from us, we now see as the path that has made all the difference. It is now the path of God's glory, the path that has given us life.

When we who have walked through the valley of the shadow of death can sincerely say in gratitude that this new path has made all the difference, we have learned to trust God again. Perhaps unwittingly, Frost has provided us a clue to trusting God again.

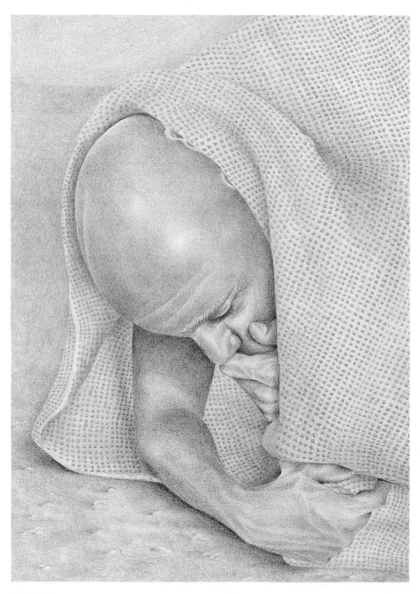

JOB 2:13
Then they sat on the ground with him for seven days and seven nights. No one said a word to him, because they saw how great his suffering was.

2

FEELING THE PAIN:
JOB'S STORY
& OUR STORY

I came to talk with my friends Tedd and Julie on a cold winter evening at their home. Before I arrived, their young son, Wes, had asked Julie whether she was going to cry when she told me the story of his brother Will. Julie said that she didn't think so. Tedd and Julie didn't cry. I did.

The story that Tedd and Julie tell is really a story of three generations, and the pain from that story sent not only a family but also a middle-size town into convulsions of grief on Easter Day in 1993. Tedd and Julie are in their early thirties. Tedd is an outgoing, goal-oriented, disciplined man, who already acts as assistant vice president at the bank and runs a family farm on the weekends. Julie is a quiet and reflective person, Tedd's high-school sweetheart, a nurturing mother and a calm and optimistic center of strength for her family and for many others.

They had family, friends, faith and focus in life. Life was going along according to their plan. That is, until April 10, 1993. Their four-year-old son, Wes, would usually accompany Tedd on Saturday mornings when he worked on the farm. Because their other son, Will, was two, he went only occasionally. But when they could join their father, they loved it. The boys *had* to dress like Dad, with boots and jeans and cowboy hats. Dad felt so proud to be initiating his sons into a world most boys do not know. Bill, Tedd's father, would meet them on the farm, and all the "boys" would work together. Their shared work was a great experience of intergenerational affection.

This day Tedd took Wes and Will to feed and tag four new calves. On the way back, his four-wheel drive became stuck in the mud, a leftover from a wet winter. They had to walk a half mile back to the farm to get Bill so he could pull them out with the tractor. Most of the way Will, riding on Tedd's shoulders, repeated, "Daddy stuck! Daddy stuck!"

They got Bill and he pulled them out. Will joined Granddad riding back on the tractor while Tedd and Wes raced ahead in the four-wheel drive. Tedd recalls waiting for Bill and Will at the farmstead, since he arrived first. He watched the tractor bounce along the rough pasture, and then, when the tractor was about ten feet away, he didn't see Will on the tractor anymore. Searching the area with his eyes, he saw Will lying face down on the ground. Will had fallen from the tractor, and it had run over him. Bill's only words were, "Oh, my God!" repeated perhaps as many times as Will's "Daddy stuck!"

They picked up Will, called 911 and rushed him to the hospital, trying to administer CPR en route. Giving him over to the emergency room staff, Tedd called Julie, tried to calm Wes, and finally they all waited. And waited. And waited.

Friends came by or happened to be there. Their pastor was at the hospital with his father, who was having some emergency medical problems. Julie arrived. No one knew what would happen, but everyone was highly agitated. Finally the word came. Little Will, age two, named after Granddad, was dead.

Shock, grief, disbelief and anguish took over. Not surprisingly, the family wanted to see Will. So Tedd, Julie and Wes, accompanied by their pastors, went in to see him. Tedd remembers the harsh, cold, sterile environment of the room. Julie recalls the perfect naturalness of Will's body. She almost said to him, "You can wake up now, buddy," as she would say to him after his nap. Tedd took his limp little hand, squeezed it, and wept. *How can I go on?* he thought.

Despite their own grief at the sudden loss of Will, their concern was for four-year-old Wes. Wes was his brother's best friend. He had seen his brother lying face down. He had literally "lost it" in the cab of the truck as they rushed to the hospital. Julie and Tedd did not quite know what to do. They also were concerned for granddad Bill. Bill was of a generation of men who rarely talked about their feelings. Granddad was silent and did not talk about the accident. Even ten months later, when I interviewed Tedd and Julie, he would not talk about it. His approach was that speaking of it with Tedd and Julie would depress *them*. It would wreck *their* evening. So Tedd and Julie were concerned for other members of their family.

Yet they also had to be concerned about each other. They had heard that nearly 75 percent of couples who lose a child eventually divorce, because the pain of the loss literally drives the parents in opposite directions. Tedd recalls sitting on the edge of their bed at 4:00 a.m. the next morning, which just happened to be Easter morning, and saying aloud, "Easter will never come for us."

The story of Tedd and Julie's first year without Will is a long one, and I will tell elements of it later in this book, but I can sum it up best by saying that they have had a most incredible network of experiences and expressions of friendship since then. Tedd recalls that one day he decided to count all the cards, letters and other expressions of affection they received. They numbered eleven hundred. To think that little Will and he and Julie and Wes had that much support was almost overwhelming.

Then there were the deepening experiences of faith. What is significant about these is that they came in such nontraditional or unexpected ways. Julie remembers a series of rich "little gifts from God" that came to them over the next several months. One day a little bunny scampered across the back yard. This was not necessarily a rare occurrence, but what happened next was. The bunny stopped, walked up to their house and looked in the window as they were looking back at it. It was almost as if the bunny somehow belonged there. Another day a beautiful butterfly appeared and rested for hours outside their bedroom window after Julie had uttered a prayer to God to send something beautiful to them that day. There was a blazing shower of meteorites one difficult night, when they couldn't sleep and looked to the heavens for some sign of divine recognition of their needs.

Tedd and Julie are faithful, strong, insightful and hopeful people. They love life and people with sincerity. They have a zest for life and family and faith and friends that is wonderful to see. They will also never forget April 10, 1993, and the devastating loss of that day. They long for Will to be back with them and with his friends. They wonder what life would have been like having him still with them. They struggle to avoid playing the "what if . . ." game. What if Will had stayed home with Julie, what if it had not been so muddy, and so on.

Tedd and Julie are now expecting the birth of another child. They have a depth and understanding that both would say was not there a few years ago. They would never want anyone to experience what they did, and they wish they hadn't gone through it. But they feel that God is good and that in his mysterious ways, God is watching over them, including Will.

Easing into the Pain of Job—My Experience with the Book of Job

Tedd and Julie's story provides the twentieth-century context for us to study Job's pain. I will describe that pain. First, however, I, Bill, must begin by telling *my* experience with the book of Job.

All of us turn to different Scriptures at different times for different reasons. For several years I was very reluctant to read, much less study, the book of Job. I was deterred for two reasons. First, I had the deeply buried fear, which I never confessed to anyone, that if I studied the book, God might bring on me, as a test of faith, some of the trials of Job. That is, since I would be trying to understand the dynamics of pain and trust, I feared that God might give me an experience of both to see if I really had learned my lesson! This is not very sophisticated, but it was my fear.

For years I was reluctant to share this story because it showed my weakness and confusion. But then, as I reflected on life, I saw that this is how most of us live our daily lives. How many people are afraid to check for abnormal lumps while taking a shower, for fear that we may discover one? How many of us refuse to look under the hood of a car for fear that we may find something that we simply do not understand? How many of us prefer not to ask or not to know when we see behavior in others that may reflect deep patterns of abuse, neglect or unconfronted pain? As humans, we willingly, even eagerly, would rather remain ignorant about huge and important areas of life than face the possible dislocation and pain of patient investigation and knowledge. So, I did not want to study Job. I would rather have remained ignorant of its lessons than perhaps open a painful journey whose start, middle and endpoint were full of uncertainty.

But I also avoided Job for a second reason: warnings from well-meaning Christians. I was told that Job's poetry was almost impossible to translate from the Hebrew, that the text was mixed up and confused, that the imagery of Job was foreign to us and that studying fifty pages of continuous poetry was too much for even the most hardy biblical scholar. Job, in a word, was too difficult to understand. It would confuse rather than enlighten me. I was encouraged to focus on biblical books that were "easier" to understand, such as the Gospels or the Psalms or the epistles of Paul. Someday, these friends told me, I would probably study Job, but for some reason *now* was not the right time.

My own fears, therefore, coupled with the warnings of others kept me from studying Job. Yet, for many years, the book still beckoned me, much like Mt. Kilimanjaro silently beckons all genuine mountain climbers or a cool mountain stream entices fly fishermen. I *knew* deeply in my heart that *someday* I would need to wrestle with Job, that *someday* I would have to try to understand its deep dynamics, that *someday* I would need to overcome my fears and launch into this great and challenging book.

Two things brought that day much closer. First, I started to see, in my own life and the life of friends, that the traditional evangelical clichés did not fit the tangled web of life's complexity. Exhortations to "seek God" when a friend was in distress or "trust God" when a friend had just lost a job began to sound empty and even judgmental. About ten years ago, when I suffered a series of personal adversities—losing my bid for an elected position, losing my job, being unable to find another position that suited my skills, and feeling a diminished sense of a focus or direction—I did not really know where to turn. I welcomed the counsel of Christian friends and the encouragement of family, but even as I received their advice, I felt very deeply that my heart concerns were not being addressed or understood. I knew that to a certain extent I had to walk the valleys of life by myself, but I desperately wanted an experienced "walking companion" who had felt deeply and expressed the pain that was so much a part of every breath I took.

Gradually my need led me to consider the book of Job. Perhaps in Job I could find a companion in my teary journey, a friend who would not simply share pain with me but would also provide the means for regaining the strength, motivation and strong center that I needed.

While I was warming up to the idea of studying the book, I was, secondly, beginning to see the person of Job in a new light. I suppose in all my years of Christian faith when I *hadn't* studied the book of Job, I saw him through the lens of the book of James, where it says, "As you know, we consider blessed those who have persevered. You have heard of Job's perseverance and have seen what the Lord finally brought about" (James 5:11).

That is, I saw Job as the example of the righteous, patient sufferer, the one who was rewarded for patient waiting. To be quite honest, that picture of Job was not very attractive to me, for I knew myself well enough to know that my first and second and third inclination in suffering would be to cry out and not to endure patiently.

So I began to see Job differently. I am not sure what specifically provoked my reevaluation of Job, but it may have been the dawning realization that the book of Job was much more than just chapters 1, 2 and 42 (the prose narration of Job's loss, patience and reward). I began to see

Job as a man who lamented his suffering, who objected to God's governance of the world and who was not afraid to let his deepest thoughts become his clearest words. I began to respect Job as a man of enormous depth of soul, of great passion and integrity, of dogged persistence and fearless single-mindedness. I saw that I needed to plunge into the book and enter its depths. I began to see that my faith now *required* me to probe it as deeply as I could. The book that I had treated with the most indifference now became the book I could not get out of my mind. I became almost as obsessed with understanding Job as Job was in understanding his pain and his God. I knew that I would not fully understand Job, but I felt very deeply that I had touched his anguish in a number of areas. My understanding would be partial, but, I hoped, it would be true.

Still, I hesitated to write, because of the following experience. I once was talking to a friend, a biblical scholar, about his writing. He was interested in writing about Old Testament personalities, and in patiently combing the Hebrew text, narrative and poetry, for every hidden jewel of insight that the text might yield about a person. He had just completed a book on David and was considering his next project. We spoke about various biblical figures—Samson, Solomon, Samuel. I suggested Saul, the first king of Israel. I will never forget his reaction. He looked at me and shook visibly and then said, "I could never write a book on Saul, for the depth of his torment is much too great for me to understand."

I felt that the depth of Job's pain exceeded my capacity to grasp and explain it, but I also felt that there were enough intersections or overlaps in understanding between Job and me that I could make it clear. My primary encouragement through all of this was the realization that Job's quest for understanding was a quest of faith, a quest which God approved (Job 42:7) and which led to a spiritually deepened, chastened and wiser Job. As I turn, then, to the description of Job's story in this and the following chapter, I do so with a sense that the suffering of Job and the pain of his life both illumine and redeem *our* suffering. Job's eventual release from pain and his learning to trust God again are signs of hope that we, too, can trust God again and rediscover the joy of life in Christ.

In the rest of this chapter I will briefly describe three things: (1) the sudden loss of possessions, family and health which Job experienced, (2) the intense cry of anguish that he uttered as a result of his loss, and (3) the attack which he feels God has made on him. As I try to understand Job's loss and his reaction to his loss, I encourage you to think about the losses you have experienced, and the ways that you have immediately reacted to your loss. Though our loss may not be as sudden, dramatic or all-consuming as was Job's, the process we go through in dealing with loss is captured perfectly by Job.

Job's Loss

As the curtain rises on Job, we find a good and honorable man presented to us. Read the first few verses of Job.

> In the land of Uz there lived a man whose name was Job. This man was blameless and upright; he feared God and shunned evil. He had seven sons and three daughters, and he owned seven thousand sheep, three thousand camels, five hundred yoke of oxen and five hundred donkeys, and had a large number of servants. He was the greatest man among all the people of the East.
>
> His sons used to take turns holding feasts in their homes, and they would invite their three sisters to eat and drink with them. When a period of feasting had run its course, Job would send and have them purified. Early in the morning he would sacrifice a burnt offering for each of them, thinking, "Perhaps my children have sinned and cursed God in their hearts." This was Job's regular custom. (Job 1:1-5)

Job cared deeply for his family. He worked industriously and was rewarded monetarily. He had the respect of the community. He honored God. He even made provisions for his children, lest they sin against God. Job is almost too good to be true. Like the fabled Richard Cory in Edward Arlington Robinson's poem, Job certainly "fluttered pulses" when he walked and "was everything to make us wish that we were in his place." His wealth and children gave him two of the triad of biblical gifts for the blessed person. All he lacked for Old Testament perfection was long life, which he had good reason to expect. The Hebrew terms for *blameless* and *upright* (1:1) stress that he, like Abraham (Genesis 17:1), would be the bearer of many blessings for the people of God.

But, as anyone who reads Jewish literature knows, whenever a Jewish story starts out wonderfully, look out! Disaster is just around the corner. So it is here. God gives permission to Satan, the accuser, to test Job's fidelity by bringing unspeakable disaster into his house.

One day when Job's sons and daughters were feasting and drinking wine at the oldest brother's house, a messenger came to Job and said, "The oxen were plowing and the donkeys were grazing nearby, and the Sabeans attacked and carried them off. They put the servants to the sword, and I am the only one who has escaped to tell you!"

While he was still speaking, another messenger came and said, "The fire of God fell from the sky and burned up the sheep and the servants, and I am the only one who has escaped to tell you!"

While he was still speaking, another messenger came and said, "The Chaldeans formed three raiding parties and swept down on your camels and carried them off. They put the servants to the sword, and I am the only one who has escaped to tell you!"

While he was still speaking, yet another messenger came and said, "Your sons and daughters were feasting and drinking wine at the oldest brother's house, when suddenly a mighty wind swept in from the desert and struck the four corners of the house. It collapsed on them and they are dead, and I am the only one who has escaped to tell you!" (Job 1:13-19)

As if these plagues were not enough, Job was afflicted with "painful sores from the soles of his feet to the top of his head" (Job 2:7). We thus have quick and debilitating disasters. In a matter of moments, Job loses his wealth, his children and his health. His wife still lives, and she counsels him to "curse God and die" (Job 2:9). God permits Satan to send the enemies of sword, fire and wind across his path. These three plagues also appear in Ezekiel's prophecy of the destruction of Jerusalem (Ezekiel 4—5) and are meant to symbolize the *complete devastation* that has taken place.

At first Job seems to accept and be resigned to his new lot. "The LORD gave and the LORD has taken away; may the name of the LORD be praised" (1:21). "Shall we accept good from God, and not trouble?" (2:10). Job suffered patiently and in silence, and it was this picture of pious, quiet suffering that no doubt influenced James as he wrote his letter.

While Job suffered silently, his plight reached the ears of his friends, and three of them came to visit him:

When Job's three friends, Eliphaz the Temanite, Bildad the Shuhite and Zophar the Naamathite, heard about all the troubles that had come upon him, they set out from their homes and met together by agreement to go and sympathize with him and comfort him. When they saw him from a distance, they could hardly recognize him; they began to weep aloud, and they tore their robes and sprinkled dust on their heads. Then they sat on the ground with him for seven days and seven nights. No one said a word to him, because they saw how great his suffering was. (Job 2:11-13)

The friends seem genuine, Job appears steadfast and all seem committed to seeing Job through this disaster.

But soon Job's firm faith is turned to fragile faith; his patient waiting to a passionate outburst and his calm acceptance into a crazed accusation. From chapter two to three there is a huge change in the way Job reacts to his condition. Many modern scholars explain this change by suggesting literary theses about Job—that chapters one and two originally circulated independently from Job 3—41 and that the tension between Job 2 and Job 3 is evidence of how badly they were put together. In my judgment, however, chapters two and three have perfect *psychological* continuity. I would like to illustrate this by a brief consideration of Emily Dickinson's poem "After great pain, a formal feeling comes."

Another Poem

In this poem, Dickinson probes the physical and psychological aftermath of great distress. She writes,

After great pain, a formal feeling comes—

The Nerves sit ceremonious, like Tombs—
The stiff Heart questions was it He, that bore,
And Yesterday, or Centuries before?

The poem teaches that after a great distress, we freeze emotionally. We become immobilized. We utter some words that are not the product of deep reflection. We seem stunned and unable to go on, but we try to do so by carrying on light or meaningless or even confused conversations. We do so in order to try to maintain a small sense of order in our lives when every other semblance of order has been turned to chaos. One person has described her anguish at losing a loved one as "feeling like wood"—hard, impenetrable, insensate.

But then, as Dickinson explores further the reaction to grief and pain, she writes,

This is the Hour of Lead—
Remembered, if outlived,
As Freezing persons, recollect the Snow—
First—Chill—then Stupor—then the letting go—

Dickinson concludes with a succession of chill, stupor, then letting go. This suggests that as we work through the early stages of our grief there is first immobility, followed by the chill and stupor that lightly cover the letting go or the expression of deep pain.

Certainly, Job felt the *chill* of great pain. In a vivid book, *Lament for a Son*, about his son's sudden, accidental death, Christian philosopher Nicholas Wolterstorff relates the indescribable pain of holding the limp body of his dead son. He described his first blast of agony as a chill, a "cold, burning pain."

Then there is the *stupor*. Job no doubt felt this state of deadened sensibility, this mental torpor, this hollowness as he sat speechless for several days in his immovable grief.

Finally, the *letting go*. I interpret this to mean the "letting go" of emotion when, for example, the heart gives itself over to grief and anguish, when the deep feelings of the soul rush out like water shot from a pressurized fire hose.

Thus, we can explain the transition between Job 2:11-13 and Job 3 as the difference between stupor and letting go, between the dead immobility that will make a person sit for seven days without a word and the torrent which breaks forth in chapter three. Pain and grief then overtake Job.

Oh, the Pain!

Starting in chapter three, Job expresses his pain. Before he ever makes a demand on God or on his friends, he expresses his agony. Though he tells his anguish throughout Job 3—31, nowhere is it more poignant or extreme than in chapter three. In this section, I will examine Job 3 in detail. This chapter is what I call Job's "prereflective" cry of pain—that is, his cry of pain *before he has had a chance to analyze it or the reasons for it*. It's like the instinctive cry of pain when we put our hand under water that is too hot, or when another person presses the sharp leg of his or her chair on our toe. The intensity of Job's loss has so overwhelmed him that all he can do at this point is scream out in agony. It's like the horrible, utterly terrifying scream of pain, loneliness and anguish of the man running along the bridge in Edvard Munch's famous 1893 painting *The Scream*. While Job was numb, in chapters one and two, he could still claim that he was basically OK ("the LORD gave and the LORD has taken away; may the name of the LORD be praised"). Now that the "letting go" has occurred, Job utters his complaint in vigorous, intense language.

Listen to some of the first anguished words of Job 3:

May the day of my birth perish,
    and the night it was said, "A boy is born!"
That day—may it turn to darkness;
    may God above not care about it;
    may no light shine upon it.
May darkness and deep shadow claim it once more;
    may a cloud settle over it;
    may blackness overwhelm its light.
May those who curse days curse that day,

those who are ready to rouse Leviathan.
May its morning stars become dark;
    may it wait for daylight in vain
    and not see the first rays of dawn,
for it did not shut the doors of the womb on me
    to hide trouble from my eyes. (vv. 3-5, 8-10)

The first several verses are almost like a reversal of Genesis 1. In those days, God created light from darkness. In this day, Job asks for darkness to come forth from the light. In that day, God blessed his work. Today, Job wants to curse God's work. Then, God created life. Now, Job wants God to take away life. Finally, in Genesis 1, creation was very good. Creation now, according to Job, is very bad. Let us return to primal darkness, Job says, and to the inchoate chaos. Let me embrace the darkness and return to the impenetrable, inky night!

Job wishes he had never been born. This is the same sentiment Jeremiah utters when he has been persecuted for preaching God's word faithfully (Jeremiah 20:7-18). It is the same lament that Faust utters in Goethe's famous play, when, after having arranged the death of his lover's brother and mother, he realizes how he has destroyed his lover. All he wants is death. Job's lament is full of the pain of life, and is uttered by a person so overwhelmed by grief that he feels nothing can reverse his condition. Better to have been stillborn than to have lived to see *this*.

Job then wonders why he came forth from the womb if he was to witness such pain. Job then begins to imagine (3:13-19) how much better death would be than life. If he were dead, he says,

I would be lying down in peace;
    I would be asleep and at rest
with kings and counselors of the earth,
    who built for themselves places now lying in ruins,
with rulers who had gold,
    who filled their houses with silver. (vv. 13-15)

He imagines himself lying down and resting in peace, in company with the kings and counselors of the earth who would provide a warm and stimulating welcome for him. Even captives enjoy ease in the peaceful and democratic realm of death (3:18). Such thoughts take Job for a moment out of his pain, like a sudden and unexpected surge of energy can make a woman ignore the agony of childbirth, or like the thought of a cold drink on a hot day provides momentary comfort for the long-distance runner.

Job has, by an act of imagination, temporarily escaped his pain. The thought of a pleasant fellowship in restful and democratic Sheol gives him relief. His relief also gives him the opportunity to raise some preliminary questions about the ways of God in the world.

> Why is light given to those in misery,
> and life to the bitter of soul? . . .
> Why is life given to a man whose way is hidden,
> whom God has hedged in? (3:20, 23)

Job's major question at this juncture is one that is increasingly asked today: *Why are those who want to die unable to do so?* Why is light given to those who long for darkness and death? It is the question of the elderly person whose body has wasted away and whose organs have given out but whose mind is clear, too clear. It is the question of the lone survivor from a Rwandan village who witnessed the most horrendous carnage all about and who herself wants to die. In Job's case, the question, of course, is, *Why don't you let me die, God?* Everyone would be better off. *I* would be in a better situation; *you* would not have to be so preoccupied with me. So let me die. Please.

These insistent questions bring the stark reality of Job's situation back to him (3:24-26). Here his pain returns.

> For sighing comes to me instead of food;
> my groans pour out like water.
> What I feared has come upon me;
> what I dreaded has happened to me.
> I have no peace, no quietness;
> I have no rest, but only turmoil.

Like a child who temporarily feels fine while he is looking away from his bloody injury only to burst into tears when he sees his hurt again, so the dramatic power of Job's pain washes over him anew. He hears his own sighs and groans again. His fears return and then, in brief, pungent and unforgettable words, he sums up his desperate condition: "I have no peace, no quietness; I have no rest, but only turmoil" (v. 26). Another translation of the last part is, "I have no rest; But trouble comes" (RSV). Perhaps as he closes his mouth, Job can see his friends fidgeting and longing to say something. When Job says, "But trouble comes," he is referring no doubt to the return of his own pain, but he also may be looking at his friends and saying, "They want to speak. This is going to be trouble." Trouble and turmoil is his present condition, and it looks like it will be his future reality.

God, the Attacker

When Job actually turns to a description of the pain he feels, he uses pictures of unforgettable power. Here is the clearest passage:

Surely, O God, you have worn me out;
    you have devastated my entire household.
You have bound me—and it has become a witness;
    my gauntness rises up and testifies against me.
God assails me and *tears* me in his anger
    and gnashes his teeth at me;
    my opponent fastens on me his piercing eyes.
Men open their mouths to jeer at me;
    they strike my cheek in scorn
    and unite together against me.
God has turned me over to evil men
    and thrown me into the clutches of the wicked.
All was well with me, but he *shattered* me;
    he seized me by the neck and crushed me.
He has made me his target;
    his archers surround me.
Without pity, he *pierces* my kidneys
    and spills my gall on the ground.

Again and again he bursts upon me;
he rushes at me like a warrior. (16:7-14)

Three words that capture Job's feeling are *torn* (v. 9), *shattered* (v. 12) and *pierced* (v. 13). He feels *torn* by the teeth of God; *shattered* by the pummeling blows of God; *pierced* by the arrows of God. Each of these words has its own particular pathos, but they all reflect the sudden violence that has come on Job. Suddenly he is torn, as by a wild beast. Suddenly he is shattered, like a plate smashed on the floor. Suddenly he is pierced by a well-aimed arrow.

A full treatment of the biblical understanding of pain is beyond the scope of this book, but it would include pictures that throw into fuller relief the desperate agony of Job. Job's pictures of pain capture his utter vulnerability and sudden helplessness. Other biblical images of torment include the sudden helplessness as well as gradual loss of control. A few other biblical images of torment are (1) sinking into the quicksand, (2) being overcome by flood waters, (3) being caught in a net and (4) being abandoned in a pit. None of these captures the sheer desperation of Job in Job 16.

The first image in Job 16 is that of being torn. God "tears me in his anger and gnashes his teeth at me." Gnashing teeth at someone is a sign of irrational anger. When Stephen, the first martyr of the Christian faith, gave his testimony about the messiahship of Jesus, his hearers could not endure his convicting and convincing words. So they "were furious and gnashed their teeth at him" before stoning him to death (Acts 7:54-58). Job feels torn apart not by people but *by God*. Nor is he torn as we would say "I am torn," meaning "I am undecided." Like a helpless animal in the clutches of a desperate, ravenous beast, he feels God's harsh strikes tearing him as though in anger.

Job also feels shattered. Shattering something is a different kind of violence than tearing something. The result is the same—things are taken apart—but to be *shattered* means to me that one is *scattered*. A shattered plate is one whose pieces I see skittering across the floor after it has been dropped. A shattered life is one in which the mind, heart and emotions are scattered and dispersed. When you are shattered, you have lost your identity, and you really cannot be put back together again by ordinary means. Little trace of your former self remains.

Finally, Job feels pierced by arrows. The arrows are a sharp, jabbing pain, a pain that simultaneously captures the violation and extremely sharp anguish of attack. In Ephesians 6 the apostle Paul describes the Christian struggle in the world and the need to equip ourselves with the whole armor of God. We are to wear that armor so that we can quench the fiery darts of the evil one—darts that are designed to pierce us. But what, pleads Job, can protect me from the *arrows of God?* What if they penetrate me? What possible defense remains for me? Christian in *Pilgrim's Progress*, that great work of seventeenth-century English Puritanism, is able to withstand Apollyon in the Valley of the Shadow of Death because he has armed himself for combat and because he does not show him his back. Fine. But what can we do when we fall into the hands of God? As the Scriptures teach, "It is a dreadful thing to fall into the hands of the living God" (Hebrews 10:31).

So Job expresses his pain, a raw, burning, wrenching pain, a pain whose sting does *not* diminish as he describes his condition to God and the readers. He is in extreme agony and bitterness also because he believes that God has singled him out for this torment. Job is no longer the quiet sufferer. He has bared his soul to God and to us. He will continue to be in agony throughout the book. It is important that we meet him in his agony now. Yet he will go much further than simply expressing his pain. For most of the book, Job is on a search for the meaning of his pain and for the God whom he feels is mercilessly tormenting him. Ultimately Job believes that there is a redemption from his pain, and he believes that he will receive an explanation from God for his pain, but it is still too early to see even the faintest glimmer of hope for Job.

A Final Word

It would be doing Job and all of us a disservice if I were now to run to Job's and our aid with comforting words. The friends tried that, and it didn't work. There is something that is so fitting and human and right in letting a person tell the full extent of his anguish without rushing in with words of comfort that surely, at this point, would be of no comfort at all. Comfort will come and new life will emerge, but not without much more agony. Job's bitter words will soon change to words of confusion and grief and anger and resignation and the darkest abandonment before he is able to see the possible good end of his great distress.

So we need to bear with Job as we bear with others in distress, or as they bear with us. Distress won't have the last word, but it will demand its due from Job and us. We give it its due by weeping with all those who are caught in the horrendous injustices of life. By weeping now, we show that we are people of compassion and hope. And compassion and hope are exactly what we need to continue Job's story.

Prayer

Our eternal God, I am like Job in so many ways. I try to live a good life, to plan for the future, to anticipate problems my children will have and to cover for them. I truly am grateful for your many blessings. Sometimes I feel that as a result of my attempted faithfulness I ought to be immune to the distresses and sufferings that happen to the rest of the world. I know I have heaved a sigh of relief when I have been untouched by sickness or tragedy. But I have learned that I cannot build an impregnable fortress around myself. Distress has come my way, through broken relationships, shattered dreams, losses too painful to enumerate. My God, all of these losses and distresses confuse and weaken me. Enable me to bring my distress to you, to describe my pain accurately and passionately, to tell you honestly about my grief. Help me continue to hope in you, though the night is long and chilly, though no apparent exit or relief is in sight. Be there for me in the darkness, and lead me into the light of your grace. Through Jesus Christ our Lord, amen.

Questions for Study and Discussion

1. Describe the loss that you, a family member or a friend has sustained.

2. Was the loss sudden or gradual?

3. Describe the pain of the loss. Which words did you and do you use to describe it?

4. Did any of the pictures of Job's distress (torn, shattered, pierced) describe your experience or the experience of your friends?

5. What would you say to Job or to anyone who describes his or her distress with phrases such as "torn to pieces," "shattered to smithereens" or "pierced by arrows"?

6. Job maintains that God is the one responsible for his loss. Is that how you see it? Why or why not?

JOB 7:7
Remember, O God, that my life is but a breath;
  my eyes will never see happiness again.

3

THE MEANING
& HEALING
OF JOB'S PAIN

T o understand someone, we must hear his or her story. As we listen, we need to be attentive to what is said and to the manner and language in which it was spoken, and even to what is felt but perhaps not voiced. Sympathetic understanding requires a big heart, a non-judgmental heart, a heart that is willing to be broken by the pain of another.

Two Brief Stories
I met Carla last year, and she opened to me a world I had only read about. She introduced me to Ron, whom we met in chapter one, and she also introduced me to the whole world of "pediatric AIDS" or, less clinically, to those children who have inherited the HIV virus from one or both of their parents. She is also one of those children.

Carla is a beautiful eleven-year-old, with the skin tone and radiance of a Kansas sunset. Her face simply glows, and when she smiles my heart wants to laugh. When she smiles, I feel that somehow the universe is a better and more harmonious place. Her illness is not in such an advanced stage as Ron's; she still runs on the track team and is an eager and bright student. She dresses up like Whitney Houston and sings in front of her mirror. She knows she is a beautiful child.

Carla was adopted as an infant. Her adoptive parents did not know that they were adopting an "HIV baby." They learned later. They felt, however, that Carla would be a special gift of grace to them, much like successful parents of Down's syndrome babies begin to see their children as special gifts from God to them.

Just recently, however, Carla's parents divorced. Whether it was the cumulative stress of urban living, the caring for a daughter they knew they would lose one day, or simply the inexplicable alienation that creeps into relationships and makes them more of an endurance test than an enduring bond, no one is quite sure. They just felt they needed to divorce.

Carla knows, however, that she has never hurt so badly in her entire life. She says that her parents' divorce is worse than HIV. She does not blame God for her situation, but she is searching for integrity wherever she goes. She feels that the world is, for the most part, made up of paid performers who are trying either to entertain us or rip us off. Increasingly she feels that her conversations are, in her words, "missing"— meaning that they just don't seem to hit the mark anymore. Carla is looking for people who understand the nature of suffering, who will not give her easy answers, and who know that life is not neat and perfect.

Carla's life has given her an insight into her own brokenness and into the brokenness of life. She is not looking for an escape from all her distress; rather, she is looking for people who will not sugarcoat life for her.

To me, Carla is a person of courage and conviction. I am humbled by her strength and honesty. She has wisdom beyond her years, perhaps because she has suffered beyond her years. She also gives us an insight into the suffering of Job, for she seeks, as does Job, the meaning of her distress and the centrality of integrity in a broken world.

We shall return to the brokenness of Job in a moment, but I would also like to illustrate the issue of brokenness on a larger scale—that of a people. I never realized how little I had really heard and understood about

Christians in the Middle East until I made a journey to Israel in May 1994. Though the purpose of the trip was to understand the peace process which came to worldwide attention through the handshake on the White House lawn between Prime Minister Yitzhak Rabin of Israel and Palestine Liberation Organization Chairman Yasir Arafat on September 13, 1993, my trip led to many other conversations and insights. A particularly moving conversation was with the Reverend Naim Ateek, pastor of St. George's Anglican Church in Jerusalem. The Reverend Mr. Ateek is a Palestinian, a native of a town now in Israel, from which he and his family were expelled in 1948. For several years he has pastored the Anglican church in East Jerusalem, a city which has been under Israeli occupation since the Six-Day War in 1967. Palestinian Arabs (Christian and Muslim) are subject to the arbitrary whims of the occupation forces.

As I tried to hear and understand Mr. Ateek's ministry, I asked him how he felt about the occupation, and how he felt about the fact that Jesus, his Savior, was a Jew, and that his current oppressors were Jews. His response is still ringing in my ears. Jesus, he stressed, understands the condition of Palestinians because he grew up in a time of occupation—Roman occupation. Jesus therefore knew what it meant to suffer humiliation, rejection, misunderstanding and persecution at the hands of an occupying force. His presence is with them today, helping them when they feel bitterness toward their oppressors by providing a sense of forgiveness, a forgiveness which really is beyond human conception. For Mr. Ateek, Jesus transcends his Jewishness and becomes the universal Savior of all those under occupation.

Listening to Job

My heart is a little bigger because I heard his story. My heart is also a little more broken. I do not look for easy and quick solutions anymore, but long for the day when Christians, Muslims and Jews can recognize and embrace their basic humanity as children of Abraham and respect the similarities and profound differences in their faiths.

It is this kind of hearing that I would like us to develop for Job. It is

a hearing that wants to try to understand Job's situation and his defini-
tion of his situation. If we hear Job, we can be confident that we are heard
also. The psalmist says,

> I love the LORD, for he heard my voice;
> he heard my cry for mercy.
> Because he turned his ear to me,
> I will call on him as long as I live. (Psalm 116:1-2)

If we want to be *heard* by God, the first step is learning to hear someone
else. If we want to be *healed* by God, the first step is learning to hear
someone else. So, we have been trying to hear Job patiently. So far we
have heard about Job's loss, his cry of pain and his deep sense that God
is responsible for the attack that has left him utterly hopeless. In this
chapter I will probe Job's pain further. My two concerns here are to study
how Job understands his pain and how his pain can be healed.

First we will study what Job thinks is the meaning of his distress. When
we suffer pain, we don't simply cry out in agony. We develop strategies
to cope with pain and explanatory mechanisms to tell ourselves what it
means. As humans we are relentless seekers for meaning. We try to
discover the meaning of someone's gestures and words to us; we search
for convincing explanations of why people act the way they do; we try
to figure out why we do the things we do. Job's special quest was to
understand his agony. We are privileged to hear both the tentative and
firm results of his quest.

But I would also like us to see, in a preliminary way, how Job's pain is
healed. The final word for Job will not be endless and agonizing suffering.
There will be redemption for him in this life. Job's healing has many
lessons for us today and is filled with some ambiguities which we will deal
with later. But it is a real healing, a healing that comes in a remarkable
and unexpected way, a healing that restores Job's fortunes and trust, and,
as such, is a healing that can help us to trust God again.

Why the Pain?

Job's pain was extreme; it was like being torn to pieces, like being smashed to hundreds of scattered fragments, like being pierced by the arrows of God. Job was like a helpless victim under the blows of a rampaging warrior (16:14). In the last chapter I explored Job's initial *feelings* relating to his pain. Here I will study Job's *thoughts* about his pain.

Job will ask, "Does this pain have any meaning?" and "Why did this pain come to me anyway?" These are natural and very human questions to pose. Did the distress arise because I did something wrong? Did it come because God is trying to send a signal to me, much like a sore muscle is a signal not to overtax the body? Is the pain a punishment or warning or something else? Job seeks knowledge because we all seek knowledge; the quest for knowledge and rational explanation is insatiable. This quest is our limited attempt to make the world comprehensible, to feel at home in the world, to feel that we not only have a role to play in this unpredictable human drama but also that we may comprehend at least a few of the ways that the world works. Our quest for knowledge is a small way of trying to redeem our human experience.

So Job will seek the meaning of his pain. I need to clarify, however, the precise question which directs Job's search. His question is *not* "Why do good people suffer and why do I suffer?" His question, rather, is *"Why am I suffering now out of proportion to my sin?"* Job's question is not about the reason for the existence of suffering; rather, it is about the *disproportionate* suffering he is experiencing. Let me explain the difference between the two more precisely.

We have learned that Job is a righteous man, a person who feared God and shunned evil. A righteous person in the Old Testament certainly knew that he was a sinner, but that his sin was covered through appropriate practice (sacrifice) and piety (just dealing and prayer). As a sinner, Job knew that he could expect the judgment of God. But because God was a merciful God, "the compassionate and gracious God, slow to anger, abounding in love and faithfulness" (Exodus 34:6), he had provided a remedy for sin. The web of Job's trust expectations, to use my earlier phrase, suggested to Job that when blessings came his way, he could expect to live and enjoy the fullness of those blessings, as long as he continued living faithfully before God. When he then experienced the tremendous dislocation and loss of family, wealth and health, Job was not simply disoriented by the loss and wracked by pain. He felt that his most basic understanding of God and God's character was at stake. Certainly he could expect pain in this life, but *this much pain?* Certainly loss is a real part of human experience, but *such overwhelming loss?* The sheer magnitude of his undeserved suffering evokes Job's visceral anger and his most profound agony. We need to understand Job's agony as *a bodily and intellectual pain.*

When Job, therefore, asks a question about the enormity of his sufferings, he is assuming one thing and questioning something else. He is assuming that God is an all-powerful God who has somehow either caused or permitted the agony to enter his life. Job will not be sympathetic with believers ancient or modern who suggest that God is powerless to stop the suffering and pain of the world or the agony of his own life. The real subject of his questioning, then—or, I may say, the question behind the question—is whether God is a just God. This is the backdrop for the entire conversation in Job. *The book of Job is an indictment of God for his supposed injustice in this instance.* In order to understand the book and Job's dilemma, we need either to feel as Job did or to be sympathetic to how a person can see the world in this way.

The agony of Job is extreme because the experience he had of loss is so contrary to everything he believes about God. Many of us have or would willingly experience pain if we believe that it is for a good reason, such as surgery to remove a tumor or chemotherapy to treat cancer. Yet Job is incensed because his loss is seemingly so disproportionate, unnecessary and out of character with what he knows of God.

Job tries to explain or come to grips with the meaning of his suffering in three ways: (1) accepting that the suffering has no meaning, (2) seeking an explanation from God, the only one who can reveal the meaning of the suffering or (3) resigning himself to his loss, while yet longing for vindication from another heavenly being, distinct from God, who will be sympathetic to his cause.

To understand Job's struggle, I need to say a few words about each of these now and then develop one or two of them later in the book.

Reaction One: Accepting That Suffering Has No Meaning

In several passages Job is convinced that his suffering has no meaning and that there can be no convincing explanation for it. To put it slightly differently, Job expresses the idea more than once that God is so powerful and we are such helpless and weak creatures that God can do anything he wants. He owes us no explanation because he is the powerful creator and we are the weak creature. God does not rule the world according to our design or desires. Since God need not give him an explanation, and since, for so long, God gives no explanation, Job concludes that God is probably not inclined to explain himself. Job must sorrowfully conclude that he will never understand his suffering.

Job can, therefore, think of nothing else but to die. We saw his cursing the day of his birth in Job 3, and he repeats the idea in Job 6:8-10.

Oh, that I might have my request,
that God would grant me what I hope for,
that God would be willing to crush me,
to let loose his hand and cut me off!
Then I would still have this consolation—
my joy in unrelenting pain—
that I had not denied the words of the Holy One.

When we humans have a crisis of meaning, we can only resolve the crisis by living in despair or by dying. One reason for the rising number of suicide attempts in our culture is that Americans are increasingly facing crises of meaning today. Why go on living if people reject me, if the future is not very positive and if I have no love at home? What purpose can my life fulfill if the relationships I've been counting on no longer work? Who, really, will miss me if I am gone? Suicide and desire for death can seem a most attractive escape for a crisis of meaning.

Job, in his crisis of meaning, asks for death. Finish the job you have started in me, O God, he says. As you have crushed me so far, now crush me to the uttermost! The apostle Paul prays for the Philippians that "he who began a good work in you will carry it on to completion until the day of Christ Jesus" (Philippians 1:6). Job prays from his agony that God who began the *bad* work in him will bring it to its logical conclusion (death) in the near future. Again Job longs for a reversal of the good order of God.

This example shows how Job's mental as well as his physical world has been turned topsy-turvy by his distress. He wants darkness, death and dissolution, for the only meaning he can extract from life now is contrary to everything he has ever believed. The pain of life has overwhelmed him. He says,

I despise my life; I would not live forever.

Let me alone; my days have no meaning. (Job 7:16)

One more example of how his pain has turned his world topsy-turvy is in 7:17-18, where he reverses the meaning of one of the most beautiful psalms. Job has accused God of being too close to him so that he can torment him. Then Job asks,

What is man that you make so much of him,

that you give him so much attention,

that you examine him every morning

and test him every moment?

Who cannot hear behind these desperate words the echo of Psalm 8?

When I consider your heavens,

the work of your fingers,

the moon and the stars,

which you have set in place,

what is man that you are mindful of him,

the son of man that you care for him? (vv. 3-4)

In Psalm 8 the author is lost in wonder, love and praise as he surveys the glory of the vast universe and realizes that human beings, such lowly and small creatures, have such an important role to play in it. In contrast, Job looks at his life and says, "Why do you make such a big deal about people?" In Psalm 8 God focuses attention on people to exalt them; in Job,

God focuses attention on people to humiliate them and drive them to despair. In Psalm 8 God's attention evokes grateful praise from the creatures. In Job 7 the attention of God yields torment. There simply may be no meaning to Job's suffering since it negates everything he has been taught to believe.

Reaction Two: Seeking an Explanation from God

Though Job asks God repeatedly to leave him alone and to let him die, he really does not want to die. Or, better said, his desire for an *explanation* from God exceeds his longing for death. For most of Job 9—31, Job seeks a direct audience with God. Throughout this section of the book, Job also speaks with his friends—Eliphaz, Bildad and Zophar. Though they try to provide a reason for Job's sufferings, Job soon dismisses these miserable counselors with anger and some cynicism ("Doubtless you are the people, and wisdom will die with you!"—12:2).

So the only person left from whom Job can seek an explanation is God himself. I, for one, am glad that Job will settle for nothing less than a divine explanation. He believes that God is ultimately responsible for his condition. He believes fundamentally that God is a good God. Therefore, God will, he believes, finally provide an explanation for his disaster.

As he thinks about demanding an explanation from God, two questions occupy Job. First, Job wonders, *Where can I find God?* and second, *How can I make my case before God?* We might think that the first question has an obvious answer. Where is God? God, of course, is everywhere. All you need to do is cry to God and He will hear. But this is an answer that is both too easy and too irrelevant for Job in his distress. Certainly God is near him, but God's nearness only intensifies his torment. Job feels he is under siege like the sea monster Leviathan, which God has created (7:12). The problem for Job is that though God is *near*, he appears not to *hear*. The heavens are like brass, and Job feels like a windblown piece of chaff. Therefore, he says,

> If only I knew where to find him;
> if only I could go to his dwelling! (23:3)

If Job could find God, he would certainly make his case:

I would state my case before him

and fill my mouth with arguments. (23:4)

Job sees himself as an attorney of sorts, preparing his case *against* God, so that when he finally has his audience with God, he can present it flawlessly. We can see Job, in our mind's eye, pacing across his room, going over all his arguments, marshaling his proofs, and already winning the argument against God. Job is like us all. When we want justice, whether with God or with another person, we prepare our case in our minds. We plan our arguments, anticipate objections, develop rebuttals and imagine ourselves winning our case by a dashing performance even before we have opened our mouths. So Job prepares his arguments.

But Job in fact really has only one question or one request to put to God. It is a simple request that he desperately hopes God will honor. He says,

Then summon me and I will answer,

or let me speak, and you reply.

How many wrongs and sins have I committed?

Show me my offense and my sin. (13:22-23)

Or, in language he speaks to his friends,

Teach me, and I will be quiet;

show me where I have been wrong. (6:24)

Job will appeal to God himself, and he will not rest until he has an answer.

Reaction Three: Resigning Himself to Loss Yet Longing for Vindication
As Job fills his mind with arguments in order to present his case to God, he achieves deeper and more penetrating insights into God and into the gospel than any other Old Testament writer. In fact, his insights arise from his pain. Pain is the crucible through which insight develops, the womb from which the new birth of understanding emerges. Job experiences wild mood swings as he seeks an explanation for his distress, and the insights he develops probe the depths of resigned pessimism as well as the heights of ebullient optimism. Pain provides spectacles by which

one may examine the depths and scan the heights of life.

First, his pessimism. In Job 14, a portion of Job's last speech in the first cycle of speeches (chapters 3—14), he sums up the insights of his previous thought. The basic point of the chapter is expressed in verse 1: "Man born of woman is of few days and full of trouble." Other biblical passages (especially Psalm 90) know the truth of the brevity of human existence, but even there the brevity of life may be redeemed by the development of wisdom (Psalm 90:12). Here, however, the realization of the short and troubled nature of life leads to a burning desire for life after death. Yet as Job 14 progresses, this burning desire is gradually quenched by the bracing waters of reality. The tree may grow again after it is cut down, but people have but one chance to live. In Job's beautiful words,

At least there is hope for a tree:
If it is cut down, it will sprout again,
and its new shoots will not fail.
But as a mountain erodes and crumbles
and as a rock is moved from its place,
as water wears away stones
and torrents wash away the soil,
so you destroy man's hope. (Job 14:7, 18-19)

The sad and plaintive cry of Job 14 and the vivid and direct question lying right under its surface ring in our ears: *Why, O God, can the tree be cut down and come back to life but not humans?* Aren't we of incomparably more value than the tree? Why, then, can't we rise again? Job's pain is leading him to insights that no other Old Testament author fully develops, insights that will only fully be developed in the New Testament.

But Job is a remarkable person, a person who simply refuses to be overcome by pessimism. Even though he cannot see the way out of his present difficulty, and even though his thoughts are often inconsistent and unsystematic, he has such great underlying strength and confidence in the basic justice of God, that hope wins out. Bright glimpses of hope shine through the book like flashes of lightning on a hot prairie night. In three passages (9:33; 16:18-21; and 19:23-27) that we will study in a later chapter, Job develops an insight and a yearning which will find fulfillment only in the life of Jesus Christ. My only purpose here is to show how his pain leads to a ray of hope.

Job knows that he needs to call on God, for only God can give him an explanation for his distress. But Job also knows that calling on God can be a dangerous enterprise. God might continue to ignore him or humiliate him or even crush him. God might not even give Job a chance to make his case. To forestall the possibility of God's potentially irrational behavior (and Job believes that God *is* acting irrationally), Job expresses his desire for an umpire or arbitrator (9:33) who would "lay his hand upon us both," that is, one who could restrain the potentially irrational conduct of God and make a just judgment in Job's favor. Thus, Job is driven to seek an arbitrator, a *second* person in heaven, because of his fear that he might not get a fair hearing with God. Once he has entertained the thought of a second person in heaven, he feels free to develop that idea. The arbitrator becomes a witness in 16:19 ("Even now my witness is in heaven") and finally a Redeemer in 19:25 ("I know that my Redeemer lives"). His confidence grows so that he can find, by Job 19, not simply a glimmer or a glint of hope, but he can discover a sure and certain confidence, a trace of "treelike" trust, that a Redeemer lives and will also redeem his sorry life.

Healing the Pain
One Sunday in worship, I heard an astonishing thing. It was during a responsive Assurance of Pardon, where the congregation repeated the words in the bulletin about the forgiveness of our sins through Christ. This particular Sunday the words were as follows: "Thanks be to God that our sins are forgiven and our future is open, through Jesus Christ our Lord." As the congregation repeated these words, I heard a man in his forties say the following, "Thanks be to God that our sins are forgiven and that our future is *over . . .*"

I knew the man. He wasn't, as far as I could tell, experiencing total Job-like loss. Yet, consciously or unconsciously, the sense of despair came to the fore and changed the word *open* to *over*. Between those two four-letter words lies the entire world.

Job, too felt that his life was over. "My days have passed, my plans are shattered, and so are the desires of my heart" (Job 17:11). Job no longer finds meaning in his life; he makes no plans for the future. But he still has energy to do one thing, and that is to seek an explanation for his suffering from God, the source of his life *and* his pain. He does not desire or expect life to return to its former glory; he just needs to pursue this one last thing before he dies. What Job and we discover, however, in the last section of the book (Job 38—42) is that though he may be finished with life and with God, God and life are *not* finished with him. Though Job thinks that he is putting his house in order, God, in fact, is building him a new house. When the darkness is impenetrable for Job, God is preparing to bring in light to obliterate the darkness.

I see Job's quest for knowledge much like Oedipus's quest for truth in Sophocles' great tragedy *Oedipus Rex*, or like Isaac Newton's or Thomas Edison's quest to understand the laws of the universe or the secrets of electricity. All these people were driven by a powerful internal desire to find an answer. Oedipus *had* to discover the truth of the plague devastating Corinth, while Newton and Edison were consumed with understanding the fundamental workings of the universe. It was said of Newton that his concentration was so intense that he could work for days or even weeks with little sleep or food. He was captivated by fundamental questions of the physical universe. I see Job as a Newtonian type of individual in the spiritual realm. Job is a dogged, brilliant inquisitor, driven by a titanic and all-consuming force to discover the basic spiritual principle of the universe by answering the question, *What kind of God rules the world?* This question and Job's experience of living have become so intertwined that they are inseparable.

But why, you may ask, isn't the traditional answer good enough for Job? Doesn't the Bible, even God's word available to Job, testify to the steadfast love and concern of God? Isn't it either a failure of faith or insufferable arrogance to pose anew the question of God's fundamental nature when the Scriptures and your earlier experience had already answered that question clearly and eloquently? God is good. God is just. Why shouldn't that settle the issue?

Job is brilliant, Job is faithful and ultimately Job becomes part of the inspired Bible precisely because he does *not* let the tradition carry him and give him the predictable and easy answer. If the answer of the tradition is not satisfying to his mind and his experience, he will rather doggedly cling to the latter than sacrifice it to the former. All advances in art, science and the deepening of spiritual insight come at the expense of traditionalists who think they know all the answers because all questions are basically easy to answer. Job is almost too much for us, conservative as we are, because he persists in asking the uncomfortable question which we only raise in a hesitating and inconstant manner when we feel we are at our boldest. Job is the most intellectually honest person I have met. Abraham may be the hero of faith for the apostle Paul, for the author of the epistle to the Hebrews and for the nineteenth-century Protestant thinker Søren Kierkegaard, but Job is my hero of faith.

But amid the bold speeches and the questioning of cherished concepts, can the person shattered by life trust God again? The Scriptures say yes. I say yes. But I add to that answer a qualification. You can be healed and trust God again, but you will be healed in a way you never imagined. Job's healing happens in Job 32—42. I will deal with that healing in much greater detail in part three, but, in concluding this chapter, I would like to show very briefly how his healing takes place. Job will be healed as he learns to hear, see and, finally, live differently.

New and Different Things for Job

Not long ago I was discussing with some students how they dealt with the issue of forgiveness. I posed the following question: "How, in fact, are you able to forgive someone? Is it simply a matter of deciding to forgive? Does the other person have to confess their fault before you forgive? Or should you wait, perhaps for many years, until God changes your heart and you feel that forgiving is not simply what you *ought* to do but something that you *feel that you must do?*"

The issue behind my questions has to do not simply with how we forgive, but also with how we are healed of grief, anger, loss or some other violation of our person. Is it primarily through an *act of our will* that healing takes place, an *act of confession or friendship* on someone else's part, an *act of God* which softens our hearts, or a combination of the three? Job discovers that it is a combination of all three which brings him back to health.

To understand the dramatic power of the varied methods used to heal Job, I would like to explore this healing in a larger literary context. One of the greatest works of Western literature is *The Iliad* by Homer. Though ostensibly about the struggle between the Greeks and Trojans over the city of Troy, it is also a subtle exploration of the causes and healing of the anger of the great Greek warrior Achilles.

Achilles is angry because the Greek leader, Agamemnon, has dishonored him. Agamemnon took Achilles' war prize from him, leaving him humiliated before all the troops. Since he is restrained from killing Agamemnon by Athena, Achilles withdraws from the battle in anger. His anger drives him to betray the Greek cause, and he sits out from the battle even as the Trojans butcher hundreds of Greeks and threaten to set the Greek fleet on fire.

Achilles will not return to the battle, the sphere of glory, until his closest personal friend, Patroklos, is killed and until Agamemnon has apologized to Achilles for dishonoring him. Although the Greeks were constantly exhorting Achilles, "Put away your anger," he could not or would not do so until his friend was killed and Agamemnon confessed his error to him. There is some question about whether Achilles' anger is *ever* really assuaged, but most scholars think that Achilles' anger goes away when he is reconciled to his friends and even to his enemies by the end of the book.

Great anger here was set aside only by the combined acts of personal decision, confession of sin by the one who dishonored him, and by the word of the gods, who disclose Achilles' fate to him. The greatest work of Greek antiquity cannot give one clear and unequivocal answer to the question of how a person gets over his anger. It is a combination of factors that leads to new life for Achilles and the Greeks.

The same can be said for Job. The interesting thing about his eventual healing is *not* that it happened at all, but that it occurred through the three means of personal decision, words of understanding from a friend, and the Word of God. This book will show how all three are important in renewing our trust in God.

Job was helped through Elihu's listening to Job (Job 32—37). The fact that Elihu listened to Job showed him that Job wasn't alone, and that the logjam of opposition between Job and his three other friends could be broken.

Job's healing resulted from his hearing of God's Word and seeing God in a new way. Before his great distress, Job felt that he knew how God acted and who God was. He had studied God's ways and been rewarded for his fidelity. He had every reason to believe that he could speak rather authoritatively about God's doings in the world. Job's disaster turned his personal world upside down. It was only when he heard God's voice in a new way and saw God differently (Job 38—42) that he could say, "My ears had heard of you but now my eyes have seen you" (42:5).

Job's healing is complete when he makes the decision to live differently (Job 42). Job makes some choices about his new life that show he is ready to live again in a positive way. He prays for his friends; he gives his daughters an inheritance; he is free to face the future with confidence.

For Job, heartache turned to healing because of all three reasons—a personal choice to trust again, a revelation of God to direct him in the path of trust, and words of a friend that help him escape the endless cycle of unprofitable conversation with other friends.

Job will trust again, and so can we. *That* is the promise of God.

Prayer

Our sovereign God, I come to you because every other refuge I have sought is weak and insubstantial. You are the God who made me, you have borne with me in my weaknesses, and you have steadily continued with me even as I have strayed from you. You are not unaware of my torment and grief, but sometimes, I confess, I feel you are indifferent to my plight. Sometimes the pain grips me and rips me and reduces me to the bare essentials of my being. Sometimes I am so weary and teary that I can no longer function. Sometimes I just want to give up. But I appeal to you and your mercy, O God. I know that I need your love and your word of explanation. I need your mercy and your presence, your blessing and your healing. Without you I am rootless, but with you I have all things. Be there in the depths of my soul and in the lilt of my laughter. Through Jesus Christ our Lord, amen.

Questions for Study and Discussion

1. Do you feel that pain simply "is," or do you think that there is a lesson or meaning in the pain?

2. What lessons have you learned from suffering?

3. Have you ever blamed God for your distress? Under what circumstances? What argument did you use?

4. How has healing taken place in your life? Who or what have been the instruments of healing?

5. How is life different for you now that you have gone through distress and have experienced some healing?

6. In which areas do you think you still need healing? Do you have any confidence that God can or will heal these?

PART 2

EXPLORING
LOSS

JOB 13:1-4

My eyes have seen all this,
  my ears have heard and understood it.
What you know, I also know;
  I am not inferior to you.

But I desire to speak to the Almighty
  and to argue my case with God.
You, however, smear me with lies;
  you are worthless physicians, all of you!

4

THE
DILEMMA
OF ANGER

I will never forget the story of Sheri. She and her husband David told
it to me late one Sunday afternoon when their four children were out
playing and the stresses of Monday morning still seemed far away.
Sheri is a woman in her late thirties, a person of great intellectual and
emotional intensity, a thoughtful, careful and caring wife, mother and
Christian friend. She has lived with her story nearly her entire life, but
only recently has she been able to tell it. The words that come to her
mouth when she tells it are *fear, pain, denial, anger, hopelessness, rejection,
betrayal* and *grief*. Hers is a multifaceted distress, and no one word can fully
capture it, but the title word of this chapter, *anger*, sums it up as well as
any.

Sheri is the fifth of six children, and was brought up in a strict evangelical home, where the father was the head of the family and church was
the focus of personal and familial life. Dad was also a part-time pastor,
and the pastor's family had the extra responsibility or duty to be a "witness" or model to the rest of the community on how a Christian family
should be. The sabbath was sacred—playing outdoors and watching TV

were not permitted—and each day started and ended with devotions.

Eventually Sheri went to the "family" college, which was in a nearby town. During the spring of her freshman year, in a sociology class, she learned two words that she had never heard before and which, for some unknown reason, terrified her. Never had she had such a reaction to learning anything. It was as if the mere mention of the words was violating her privacy very intensely. The words were *rape* and *incest*. She took her troubles to the local pastor and confessed that something like this might have happened to her in her home as a girl. Her memory was cloudy, but something very wrong had happened at home, she felt. She needed help to explore her vulnerable feelings. Instead of keeping her revelations private, the pastor, who was a friend of Sheri's parents, told them, and they immediately withdrew Sheri from college.

She spent the next few months in Christian counseling, but as Sheri tells it now, the purpose of the counseling seemed to be for her to forgive and forget whatever wrong things she felt were done to her in the past. She talked with her father, and they both agreed to forget the past, forgive whatever had occurred and move on to the future. She forgave because, as she tells it, "He asked my forgiveness, which I gave mostly because I didn't feel I had a choice. After all, if God taught it, I was to do it." Case closed. So it appeared.

Only several years later, when Sheri and David's daughter was about four years old, did old memories begin to surface for Sheri. This time they were ghoulish and extreme. "I would awaken—that is if I ever got to sleep at all—with feelings of being smothered by a weight on my chest. I wouldn't be able to breathe. I couldn't stand to be touched even by my kids. I knew I needed help fast." She began to remember quite precise instances of being sexually abused as a child.

She received counseling help again, this time to understand the full meaning of the vivid memories that were surfacing. She remembered that she had been sexually abused by four different men or boys, all members of her extended family, that this abuse had happened dozens of times over several years, and that all of it was supposed to have been forgiven and forgotten because of her having accepted her father's "confession" when she was nineteen years old. At this time Sheri's feelings of anger, guilt, vulnerability and hopelessness began to dominate her life.

"Emotionally, the scars were very deep and very serious," says Sheri. "I felt totally worthless and dirty. I felt violated and evil. I was consumed by guilt and hopelessness. I felt that I had done some evil, horrible thing and God was punishing me. *I must have been a terrible, appalling person for God to have allowed this to happen to me.*"

Sheri became suicidal and was hospitalized. She felt trapped, tormented and listless. David recalls that when he tried to touch her it was like touching an iceberg. At the advice of her counselor, she began to keep a diary. What was there to lose? All seemed utterly hopeless. "My emotions during these months were crazy. I was on a roller coaster that wouldn't stop. Self-destructive thoughts and feelings sometimes were acted out in hurting myself physically or emotionally."

Her church, a different church from the one in which she had grown up, was not particularly helpful. Sheri says that its approach to injury was "forgive, forget and go on." She remembers distinctly that people from the church gave her six months to get her life in order—to recover from the effects of her remembered abuse and return to all the normal duties of a wife and mother. When Sheri was unable to resolve the violations within that time, the church people began to tell her she was neglecting her children, husband and duties as a church member. They gradually withdrew their offers of child care and their personal support. Finally their support stopped completely.

Since that time David and Sheri have made several decisions—to move to a new town, to join a new church—but the major breakthrough for Sheri has been, in her words, "to trust my own experience of things." She was raised to believe her experience should be subordinated to her parents' interpretation of Scripture and life. For a long time she felt that she had to sacrifice *her* felt experience of life because God and Dad (who could not be easily separated in her experience or memory) had to be right.

Now she no longer believes that. She knows that her experience is real.

81

She knows that she was treated unjustly. She knows the pain, anger, dislocation and despair that have been part of her life. All these things are TRUE, capital letters.

So where does that leave God? And family? And church? And trusting again? I had to ask her those questions, because we both knew that she had to answer them. Her first response was, "It is so slow and it is so difficult!" It was like rebuilding a home that had been devastated in a tornado. Then she spoke in sure and measured tones, and said that she is no longer a fearful person. She has been through hell and survived, and though the anxieties persist, she isn't afraid to speak to people or make decisions. She wants to return to school to get a master's degree. Her motivation to live and make her own decisions is very strong. She is beginning to speak about her past with openness and candor.

God is there, but Sheri is not fully convinced that God is good. But for the first time in her life, she doesn't feel bad about not being sure whether God is good. She says it briefly: "If God is good, he will be there for me in the future, and he will show it to me." There is a bit of defiance and boldness and some anger in her voice, but it is the defiance of Job, the defiance of the one who is willing to be wooed again but is not going to be sold an easy answer or a pious platitude.

Reconciliation with family and church will be much more difficult. Sheri feels that her family is a bit afraid of her because of her newfound freedom. They really don't know what to make of her. She believes that healing is taking place there, but it is the healing that comes from a person who believes she is stronger and able to walk on her own. Anger remains, and tears are not exhausted, but Sheri and David feel that something stronger has emerged in Sheri's life, and they are grateful. May Sheri's story remain with us as we reflect on Job's and our anger.

Reflecting on Anger
Harriet Goldhor Lerner opens her bestselling book *The Dance of Anger* with the simple observation, "Anger is a signal, and one worth listening to." Just as shortness of breath may signal heart problems or a flashing yellow

light signals construction ahead, so anger is a signal or tip-off to something else. Anger is like a signpost, or a directional arrow, that points beyond itself to something else. It is to be taken seriously for itself, but we also need to recognize that it is pointing to something else, something less tangible but no less real.

We all have stories from our experience about the place of anger in our lives. If you are a woman, the chances are good that you have learned that feeling and expressing anger are not encouraged. As Lerner says, "Sugar and spice are the ingredients from which we are made. We are the nurturers, the soothers, the peacemakers, and the steadiers of rocked boats. It is our job to please, protect, and placate the world" (p. 2).

Anger is not within the repertoire of the woman who wants to please. If a woman expresses her anger she is often dismissed as irrational or as a complainer. Our society sends clear messages that anger, for at least half of its members, is not OK.

If you happen to be a male in our culture, society sends out a different message: for you anger is unavoidable, but still unacceptable. Males, we are told, are aggressive by nature and must have outlets or channels for their energy and anger. The typical channels for anger and rage are athletics and work with one's hands. Hit the punching bag and not another person, we say. Pound with the hammer on wood and not with your fists on another person! We are warned that unless we teach men how to channel their anger, we are nurturing our own destruction as a society. We even explain the high incidence of males in prison as a function of how men have reacted to situations that made them angry. Men in prison are those who have not learned how to control or channel their anger.

Both of these scenarios reflect society's attitude toward anger and the proper expression of it. For one group, women, anger is not permissible. For another group, males, anger is unavoidable but still unacceptable. In the case of the women, the anger must be suppressed. In the case of the men, the anger *cannot* be suppressed, so either they learn to channel the anger or *they* will be suppressed. In both instances anger is perceived as a terribly powerful and sometimes unavoidable force that must be kept in check for the good of society and the stability of our families. Anger, we think, has a very destructive aspect to it.

As we look at the experience of Job and review the contours of our lives, we discover just how prevalent anger is. Job's anger at his friends and God is clear. Who can't see the seething anger of Job toward his so-called comforters when he says,

A despairing man should have the devotion of his friends,
even though he forsakes the fear of the Almighty.
But my brothers are as undependable as intermittent streams,
as the streams that overflow. (Job 6:14-15)

A stream that may not be flowing in a desert land is the worst kind of stream. When Job needs their help the worst, his three friends cannot be counted on to provide cool, soothing words.

Job is also angry at God, a point I will develop in detail, principally because Job believes that God has, for no good reason, brought this great affliction on him.

What should our approach to Job's anger be? Should we say that it is illegitimate because, as the Scriptures teach, "Do not let the sun go down while you are still angry"? (Ephesians 4:26). Some scholars suggest as much when they say,

Job felt deep anguish and bitterness, and he spoke honestly to God about his feelings to let out his frustrations. If we express our feelings to God, we can deal with them without exploding in harsh words and actions, possibly hurting ourselves and others. (*Life Application Bible*, p. 851)

That is, it is all right to be honest with God, but by all means keep it rational and calm! Don't speak your anger.

I suggest a different approach—one informed by the book of Job and by the nature of anger itself.

First, as we look at the book, especially the last chapter, note that God commends Job's speech. In verse 7 of chapter 42 God says, "I am angry with you and your two friends, because you have not spoken of me what is right, as my servant Job has."

God's judgment on the friends and his blessing of Job is because of proper or improper speech. Job's speech is commended. Job spoke correctly of God. The angry one was the one who spoke "what is right." Rather than referring only to Job's confession in the last few chapters of Job, I take this to refer to the *general tenor of Job's words throughout the book*. If so, then God is *commending* Job's complaint and Job's anger. God can take it! As a matter of fact, God is saying here that it was right for Job to have said what he said. There is nothing said by God about how Job's anger might have possibly hurt himself and others.

Second, the nature of anger argues that anger should be expressed. Anger, in my approach, is something like thirst or hunger. It is not necessarily right or wrong; it just *is*. We may know that there are certain activities that habitually provoke anger (just as jogging will habitually provoke thirst), but to blame a person for getting angry is, to me, similar to blaming a person for having a cavity in his or her teeth or having to blow one's nose when one has a cold. Anger is one of the constellation of emotions and feelings that mark us as being human.

So to help us understand our own anger and Job's anger and see Job as a wise guide or sage counselor about our anger, I will concentrate on three ideas: (1) thinking about our anger, (2) understanding Job's anger and (3) drawing lessons about anger.

Thinking About Our Anger

Our anger may be caused by many things, but in my judgment, it arises from two major sources: from a gap between expectations and reality and from our feeling of injury. When I speak of a gap between expectations and reality, I mean the disappointment and pain that result from promises that are not fulfilled or plans not carried out. Disappointment and pain do not always lead to anger; they can lead to dejection, depression and despair, but they are often expressed in angry thoughts, words and actions.

A young man was describing to me the anger and resentment he felt growing up in an alcoholic family. At times he felt that since he had no other family with which to compare it, his family was normal. Yet he could barely suppress his rage as he talked to me. His father would be "sick" for many days in a row. Afterward he would promise to make it up to his son and his daughters by taking them to a ball game or bringing them unspecified presents. The young man told me of how many times he went to bed expecting to hear good news the next day—that they actually were going to a game together with their father—but the good news never came. Dad was sick again or had to do something and so could not be with the children. The boy's disappointment turned to resentment and anger; the gap between expectation and reality was so painfully wide.

Anger also comes our way when we have suffered injury. This injury may include bodily harm, but is certainly not limited to it. It includes our anger when we lose a loved one or our pain when humiliated by another.

I could feel the anger of a young woman, recently divorced, as she described to me the crude way that her ex-husband had dumped her, the twenty-four-hour-a-day responsibilities she now had for the children, the difficulty in getting child-support payments from the father, the poverty she had been reduced to. She would angrily deny that she was angry. She would deny that *he* was still running her life and "pulling her chain." She claimed that she couldn't be happier living on welfare, but the fact that she brought up her "joy" in every conversation I had with her made me wonder. Her experience of painful divorce made her think that the whole world was arrayed against her. When a policeman stopped her, it was definitely harassment; when she didn't get a job it was because it was a "man's world"; when someone was brief with her, it was their attempt to ruin her life. My friend had been badly injured and was a seething caldron of rage.

You don't need to have experienced these things to know the reality of anger. Many of us live with anger, and it silently corrodes our creativity and turns us into sullen, pessimistic, intolerant people. Because anger is such a "no-no" in our culture, we have learned to conceal and deny its presence with us.

I was never so aware of how much anger and denial play a part in my life as just recently. I (Bill) am a large man, over six foot two, and I should weigh about 200 pounds. I weighed 200 pounds several years ago. Recently I became disheartened because I seemed unable to drop my weight under 215 pounds. But then denial entered. I began to buy clothes that were too tight, because I told the salesperson that I anticipated losing weight and it wouldn't be good to buy clothes that would be too big for me. Then I remember walking into my bathroom without my shirt on and staring at myself in the mirror for several minutes from several angles until I had *convinced* myself that I was still very trim. Finally I became angry with myself, vowed to change my eating and exercise habits and, to prove my sincerity, had a few cookies—which I would be swearing off of as soon as I finished them!

We deny things that are not socially acceptable, and anger is certainly one of those things. We say we are "thinking" when we are feeling spiteful, "busy" when we are livid and "constructively critical" when we want to destroy someone else's ideas. We plot revenge and think of the many ways that we can make someone else's day as miserable as they have made ours. Sometimes we appear unruffled and seemingly imperturbable, and sometimes we can barely manage to remain civil. But anger, pure and simple, is running and ruining our lives.

The purpose of this chapter is to show that anger *was* a major reality for Job in his distress and that anger, though it embittered and used him, was helpful in discovering his true complaint and, ultimately, in trusting God again. Through repeated expressions of anger, Job came face to face with the nub of his problem and with his God. Anger kept him searching for justice, yearning for release, longing for honesty and seeking for God. His anger, I believe, was an expression of faith and faithfulness, for through anger he would not let God go. Through anger he demanded (and got) a response from God. Through not *deselfing* himself (a word used by Lerner to describe the way people frequently do not face their anger or confront its source), Job was most human and most faithful. Through anger, Job, in God's words, "[spoke] of me what is right" (42:7).

Understanding Job's Anger

It will be helpful to divide this section further into the *causes*, the *contours* and the *conclusion* of Job's anger. I want to determine the reason for Job's anger, the various ways he expresses his anger and the way that he, as it were, sums up his anger to God. We will study the text of Job closely and then make applications to our lives in the final section of this chapter.

The *cause* of Job's anger is that he feels God has brought this great distress on him and that he thinks his friends are unsympathetic to his plight. We will examine his relationship to his friends in a later chapter. Even if Job had known that Satan, the accuser, was really the immediate cause of his suffering, he would have been unwavering in his accusation of God. In the words of one commentator, Job is a "radical monotheist." That is, Job believes that every aspect of life is ultimately controlled by God. The advantage of this position is that he knows who is precisely responsible for the misery he experiences. His belief in God doesn't permit him to blame a lesser being (Satan); it doesn't allow him to say that some areas are outside the control of God (e.g., natural law). God is a very personal God who must have been personally behind the scheme to bring misery on Job. Make no mistake; God has *caused* Job's pain.

The strength of this belief propels Job to seek his God and express the *contours* of his anger. God, in Job's judgment, has attacked, shattered, burst in on, pierced, destroyed, crushed and haunted him. In the unforgettable language of Job 16,

All was well with me, but he shattered me;

he seized me by the neck and crushed me. (v. 12)

God gave Job no rest and continued to torment him in many ways. God is the source or cause of his great distress; God, therefore, must be addressed if he wants his distress alleviated.

Job feels that God has ruined his life, and Job is angry about it. Everything was going fine. All were happy, prosperous and religious. For some unspecified reason, disaster befell his family. After his agonized cry (Job 3), he thinks about his loss and the nature of the God who caused this to happen.

God's Irrational Anger

Interestingly enough, the way Job thinks of God is that *God is possessed by inexplicable anger*. Anger, Job says, is what is really motivating God:

God assails me and tears me in his anger
and gnashes his teeth at me;
my opponent fastens on me his piercing eyes. (16:9)

Job feels that he faces God not just as an opponent, but as an enemy, receiving divine wrath:

His anger burns against me;
he counts me among his enemies. (19:11)

Job, in a huge leap of logic and history, claims that anger has been one of God's most characteristic features since primitive times:

God does not restrain his anger;
even the cohorts of Rahab cowered at his feet. (9:13)

This refers to the ancient sea battle between Yahweh and Rahab, a beast of the deep—a battle that took place as part of the fashioning of creation from chaos. In Job's mind God is not simply having a bad day; he has been driven by anger since the beginning of time. Anger is an essential element of his personality—just as it is now an abiding element of Job's nature.

But finally Job returns to God's anger today, wishing that it would be stayed and that he would be protected from it:

If only you would hide me in the grave
and conceal me till your anger has passed! (14:13)

Job hopes that God is strong enough to put his anger aside for now.

God's Moral Indifference

In addition to attributing anger to God, Job accuses God of being morally indifferent. This accusation also flows from Job's personal experience. After all, Job was a righteous man and is now being attacked by God. This *must* mean that God's value system is skewed! So Job asks a series of rhetorical questions to his comforters and to God, expecting the answer "not often" or "never" to his first questions.

Yet how often is the lamp of the wicked snuffed out?
   How often does calamity come upon them,
   the fate God allots in his anger?
How often are they like straw before the wind,
   like chaff swept away by a gale?
It is said, "God stores up a man's punishment for his sons."
   Let him repay the man himself, so that he will know it!
Let his own eyes see his destruction;
   let him drink of the wrath of the Almighty.
For what does he care about the family he leaves behind
   when his allotted months come to an end? (21:17-21)

Job's anger at God's moral indifference goes even further. Job does not simply want to make an *observation* about God's style. He wants, as it were, to make God face up to it. God is not simply indifferent to the plight and claim of the just; he is actively working against justice. Note Job's bitter words in chapter 9:

It is all the same; that is why I say,
   "He destroys both the blameless and the wicked."
When a scourge brings sudden death,
   he mocks the despair of the innocent.
When a land falls into the hands of the wicked,
   he blindfolds its judges.
   If it is not he, then who is it? (vv. 22-24)

The terrifying thought behind these verses is that God actively works to harden the heart and to blind the eyes of those who are charged with justice in such a way that the wicked prevail. All of this flows from Job's own experience of loss:

Does it please you to oppress me,
   to spurn the work of your hands,
   while you smile on the schemes of the wicked? (10:3)

God has turned the world upside down for Job; that must mean, Job reasons, that the entire world, in fact, has been turned upside down. God is doing things that are morally indefensible.

Job's Moral Purity

Job's anger rages on. He turns from accusation against God to a consideration of his own situation and needs. He has no doubt that, in this situation, he is in the right. To his comforters he says,

Relent, do not be unjust;

reconsider, for my integrity is at stake. (6:29)

Or, as another translation says, "my integrity is still intact!" (David Clines, *Job 1—20*, p. 156). He laments his current condition to anyone who will listen:

I have become a laughingstock to my friends,

though I called upon God and he answered—

a mere laughingstock, though righteous and blameless! (12:4)

Job's righteousness in the midst of the unjustified divine attack has exacted a huge toll on him; yet he tries to remain strong. In the words of William Ernest Henley's poem "Invictus," Job could say, at this point,

Under the bludgeonings of chance

My head is bloody, but unbowed.

Job's own words capture his sorry situation:

My face is red with weeping,

deep shadows ring my eyes;

yet my hands have been free of violence

and my prayer is pure. (16:16-17)

Because Job is convinced of his own purity and uprightness, that he has done nothing deserving this sort of punishment, he, though weak, feels he is in a strong position to ask God for a reason for his suffering. Job first asks his friends to show him the error of his ways (6:24) but, when they cannot, he turns and makes the same request of God:

How many wrongs and sins have I committed?

Show me my offense and my sin. (13:23)

But God is silent on this issue for now. Job will have to live for a while with the *lack* of divine clarification.

Just because God will not answer Job's request does not mean that God is absent. As a matter of fact, Job's anger and desperation increase precisely because God continues to hound and oppress him. That is, Job's anguish and pain grow with no relief in sight, and God remains near and simply does nothing about it! God *could* do so much to remedy his situation, Job thinks, but all God does is increase Job's torture. God has become, in one scholar's words, an oppressive presence who turns on the whirlpool of torment full blast! God *could* do so much, but since he does not, he must be held morally responsible for the sorry condition on earth and, in particular, the sorry situation of Job!

Job is certain that death will come for him soon and that he therefore has nothing to lose. So he goes right to the throne of God with his pain:

Am I the sea, or the monster of the deep,   •

    that you put me under guard?

When I think my bed will comfort me

    and my couch will ease my complaint,

even then you frighten me with dreams

    and terrify me with visions. (7:12-14)

Waking or sleeping, Job is haunted by the unrelenting presence of God.

Will you never look away from me,

    or let me alone even for an instant?

If I have sinned, what have I done to you,

    O watcher of men?

Why have you made me your target?

    Have I become a burden to you? (7:19-20)

To make his complaint even more vivid, we should translate 7:19 as the Revised Standard Version and many scholars do:

How long wilt thou not look away from me,

    nor let me alone till I swallow my spittle?

Though we might wish that Job had used other words, this vivid expression captures the intense preoccupation of God with Job. Job is nearly dead, but God continues to torment him:

Will you torment a windblown leaf?

    Will you chase after dry chaff? (13:25)

It just doesn't add up for Job. God created him, loved him, blessed him with so many things, made him a pillar of the community and an exemplary man of faith, and now God seems determined to destroy him.

Your hands shaped me and made me.

Will you now turn and destroy me? (10:8)

Job is left with a real dilemma. He needs God to answer him and clarify his pain and anger, but God seems determined to hurt him. He is in a theological catch-22: Job must ask for help from his destroyer.

Leave Me Alone, Please

This dilemma drives Job to a contradictory approach: he wants God to leave him alone *and* he wants an audience with God. Harassed by the pain, stung by the divine betrayal, miffed by the rejection of friends, humiliated in front of servants, dishonored, distressed and dismayed, driven by anger, unable to see any way out of his gloomy situation, Job asks God to leave him alone. In verses unique in Scripture, Job begs for relief from God's presence *so that he might have a moment of joy.* Note the pathos of Job's words:

Are not my few days almost over?

Turn away from me so I can have a moment's joy

before I go to the place of no return,

to the land of gloom and deep shadow,

to the land of deepest night,

of deep shadow and disorder,

where even the light is like darkness. (10:20-22)

This desire (see also Job 7:16) reflects Job's hopelessness, his sense that life is over, that he never again will see good. Job's anger has been transmuted into despair and resignation, because he can see no way out of his dilemma, and all other suggested avenues (such as confession of sins, as the comforters suggest) are intellectually and spiritually unsatisfying. He despises his life and wishes for a hastening of his few remaining days. As Job says,

What strength do I have, that I should still hope?

What prospects, that I should be patient? (6:11)

Remember, O God, that my life is but a breath;
   my eyes will never see happiness again. (7:7)
My spirit is broken,
   my days are cut short,
   the grave awaits me. (17:1)

How Anger Leads to Hope

Yet Job's anger will not let him permanently remain in despair. Though he speaks out of the anguish of his spirit (7:11), and though all hope appears to have disappeared, Job will not give up. Something drives him on. I believe that this is Job's deep sense that despair, pain and hopelessness are *unworthy* of the God he had been serving. His God is, in fact, not a God who is a destroyer. Job's spunkiness, persistence and raw challenge to God arise from a settled conviction that the universe requires a God of justice at its very core. But *this* God, in Job's mind, has a lot of explaining to do. Therefore, Job must seek an audience with God.

Oh, we may say to Job, you have gone too far! Why not submit to God and realize that "God is his own interpreter and he will make it plain"? Why not patiently and quietly accept your lot, knowing that God will bring things to a just conclusion someday? Why all the noise and ruckus? Isn't there virtue in suffering in silence, like lambs led to slaughter, like the Lord Jesus Christ who complained not at all and went to judgment with silence on his lips?

Perhaps there is. But for Job to suffer in silence would be tantamount to suffering without integrity. To suffer silently would mean that he would be indifferent to the question of whether the universe has a firm moral foundation. Some may keep their pain and confusion to themselves, but for Job the unanswered questions and contradictory feelings are so intense and so all-consuming that he must say what is on his mind. There really is no acceptable substitute. Job feels that God needs to be accountable to the creature, even though Job doubts whether God sees it that way.

The reason that Job will take his case to God is that "there is hope for a tree" (14:7). Nature, observes Job, renews itself; a tree can grow even after it has been cut down. If nature can do this and if, as the Bible teaches, we are of much more value than trees and other living things, doesn't it seem reasonable that there is hope for us? Job does not develop the idea fully that this hope is an *eternal* hope; so there must be something else *here* and *now* that will happen for our good. Hope and despair are mingled expressions of Job's anger.

As Job *concludes* his anger, then, he does so by presenting his case before God. He fills his mouth with arguments; he makes the case of the tree. He wants a hearing and he wants vindication. So sure is he of the rightness of his cause that he says,

Oh, that my words were recorded,

that they were written on a scroll,

that they were inscribed with an iron tool on lead,

or engraved in rock forever! (19:23-24)

He wants the whole world to hear his complaint. He has done all that he can. The ball is in God's court.

Four Lessons About Anger

I was brought up to think that anger was destructive and counterproductive. Anger was something I was supposed to *overcome*. With suitable maturity in Christ I would soon learn, I thought, not simply to control my temper but even to moderate my feelings of anger.

Then I read the book of Job and got to know Job closely. If Job were alive today, he would be able to give us some valuable advice on anger. I think that he would be able to teach us at least four things.

First, Job would say that anger is often an expression of faith. Like others, Job was angry principally because he *did* believe, deep down, that God is a just and good God and that therefore what happened to him was unjust and should be rectified. To be angry means that we still believe. Anger is one of the strongest motivators for change in our lives and society because the message of anger is that everything *ought not to be* the way it is. It would be hard to imagine the massive political changes in South Africa

95

in the last few years without the years of anger on the part of blacks *and* whites, dating from the beginnings of the apartheid system and refined by the Sharpeville massacre, the Soweto killings, the outlawing of the African National Congress and continuing through the release of Nelson Mandela from prison in 1991. It will be hard to imagine creative political change or spiritual deepening in our hedonistic and materialistic culture without the anger of people who believe that our country still needs to live up to its basic affirmation of liberty and justice for all. Anger kept Job going, even when he could have sunk deeply into silent and sullen despair.

A second lesson is that we ought to speak honestly to God of our anger. Job spoke his anger honestly. Even though he was, at times, guilty of rash and presumptuous speech, God praised him in the end because he spoke what was right. A corollary to this is that we ought not to be excessively concerned if we overstate our animosity or other feelings while we are speaking to God. God can take it!

Some of the prayers I remember the most are the excessive ones I have uttered. I remember several years ago when I was a finalist for a pastoral position which I thought was right for me. I was scheduled to visit the committee late in April. The day before I was to depart, I came down with pneumonia. In the past twenty years it was the only time that I have missed work or something as important as an interview because of sickness. The interview was rescheduled for two months later and, I believe, after the final decision had already been made. In my prayers during that season I accused God of undermining me and deliberately getting my hopes up only to dash them. I told him that I felt betrayed. I wondered aloud what he thought he was doing by tormenting me. It was not a pretty prayer. Yet it did lead to something in my case, and that something is a third point which Job would explain to us about anger.

Job would say, third, that God will respond to our anger. Often the response is not what we expect, but he will answer. Sometimes I believe that God desires our earnestness, anger and imagination more than our correctness or politeness. I was talking to a prominent retired publisher of a chain of newspapers in the Midwest about the characteristics he was looking for in a reporter. Without hesitation, he stressed that the two most important traits for a good reporter were enthusiasm and imagination. Before I conceded the point, I asked him about other characteristics. What about intelligence? What about a good writing style? Literacy? Politeness? Wouldn't enthusiasm get the paper into a lot of difficulty if it wasn't channeled correctly? He responded by saying that the other things can be taught, but he had no idea about how to generate enthusiasm and imagination. Without these, the paper and the people working for it have no commitment or reason for being.

Imagination and enthusiasm generate a response from people. Why would we think it would be different for God? Job is one of the most imaginative people of the Old Testament; in his speeches he explores depths and themes that are not surpassed theologically until the New Testament. He is also enthusiastic, though we have called Job's enthusiasm by other names: stubbornness, doggedness or impertinence in insisting on a response. These are all different ways of saying that Job was *enthused* (literally, "indwelt by a god") as he made his case. Job would teach us to express ourselves without reserve to God, for the imagination and enthusiasm needed to do this prepares us to hear a word from God, and that word for Job, and probably for us, was different from what he expected.

Finally, Job would probably caution us about our expression of anger. He would teach us that from his experience the angry person alienates people. Job's passionate outbursts were not a problem to God, but they were problematic to others. Job's comforters were people steeped in the religious traditions of the day, and they were pretty sure they knew how God worked. It is no different with us today. Those in prominent religious positions in our society have a vested interest in believing that God works in certain ways, especially ways that would not catapult them from their lofty positions. Our anger often closes us off from them.

When Job refused to accept the religious people's explanation of his catastrophe, he became dangerous to them. Job upbraided them for their lack of compassion and their arrogant claims of wisdom, thereby alienating himself from them. I think, by and large, that this is the way things work today. Expressions of anger are usually taken at face value by those who hear them. They do not try to see how this might point to something deeper. The expression of anger so alienates people that the angry one is often left alone with his or her thoughts.

It would not be honest to claim, therefore, that the expression of anger only has positive results. We wish that people could be as strong, understanding and encouraging as God. Yet neither Job nor we find that to be true. I close this chapter with a dilemma that I cannot fully resolve. To be honest and angry with God can be a vital and powerful expression of faith; to do the same with people can bring loneliness and isolation. Which will we sacrifice? Our experience suggests we ought to control our anger; Job's suggests that we ought to express it. This is a true dilemma of faith, one which is resolved through discussion and prayer, with firm reliance on Jesus Christ.

Prayer

O eternal God, who created me with enormous capacities for good and evil, hear my prayer. Anger, I confess, is so much a part of my life. Sometimes it is righteous and healthy anger, I am sure, but other times it seems to dominate my thoughts and leave me helpless. Because of my anger, I contemplate revenge, I am short with people, I do not even like myself. Often, my God, I am angry at you for giving me the life I now live. I would change so many things, but I feel powerless to do so. If I express my anger, I fear that I will lose my friends and family. If I conceal it, I feel that I may lose my soul. I sometimes feel wretched because of this, and I need you more and more. Bring order and clarity to my jumbled mind, and bring grace and love to my actions so that, armed not simply with anger but with your power and love, I may meet the challenges of the day and all days with the help of my Savior, Jesus Christ the Lord, amen.

Questions for Study and Discussion

1. What were you taught about expressing anger as you grew up?

2. What is your attitude about anger today?

3. What do you think about Job's overstatements, such as how hurtful his comforters were or how he felt God had attacked him?

4. What things about the world or your own life anger you now?

5. What do you plan to do about them?

6. How would you handle the dilemma with which this chapter ends?

✳ JOB 17:11
My days have passed, my plans are shattered,
and so are the desires of my heart.

5

A TALE
OF TWO
GRIEFS

G rief is such a personal thing. It is unique to each individual. Yet there are some common threads that run through the experience of grief, like streaks of red through many Scottish tartans. To understand Job's lament, we must first be able to identify, confess and own our own grief. In this chapter both of us, Glandion and Bill, will share with you some of our encounters with grief, and then we will try to understand Job's grief. By looking at our stories and Job's story, we would like you to consider your own thoughts and experiences of deep sadness.

Grief is our common experience; even Jesus was known as the "man of sorrows and acquainted with grief." Through our study of grief, may we learn to cast our cares on Christ, the one who has borne our griefs and our sorrows.

Glandion's Grief: Pain and Sorrow

The grief that I am facing as I write this is that I have lost three dear friends in the past year. All were men who played a unique role in my life; all are utterly irreplaceable. I think of them when I read and pray and minister. Sometimes I even reach for the phone to tell them of a discovery I have made, as I did for years, but then I catch myself and know that Al, Robert and Tom will never again be on the other end of the line.

Their loss has left me with a deep pain, like an internal itch that cannot be scratched, like a rash that will not go away, like a cut that resists every effort to salve it. I feel that love is such a *damnable* thing sometimes. If I do *not* love, I become lonely and isolated. But now I am realizing how much I have to lose if I *do* love. I entered into relationships with these men freely, but they have all ended against my will. I am left with such a hollow feeling, a sense that there is a gaping hole at the center of my being. Things are so final, and I wonder if I should ever take the risk of loving again. Let me tell you a word about each man, as a tribute to them and as a comfort for my own grief.

I met Al when I was in high school. He was several years older than I and had a physical disability, but we soon developed a friendship that made our differences insignificant. We met at church, and he took me under his wing and became my mentor in faith and life. He was the first man I knew who affirmed the importance of my mind, the power of ideas and the value of well-chosen words. He was more of a confidant than a role model for me. We would go on trips together and not speak for hours, but then the thoughts and insights would come with the emotional and intellectual intensity of a summer storm on the prairie. We would read and discuss and dream and connect at levels that I never thought were possible. He was so much to me. Aristotle has said that friendship is when a single soul dwells in two bodies. I felt that way about Al.

I remember standing at his grave a few months ago. I recalled the pain I felt at his burial. I knew that never again, in this life, would I have the sweet intimacy of his company. I thought of his death, and then I thought of my own mortality. I wondered whether I really had the energy or interest to pour myself into another person, as Al had done with me. I left the cemetery that day absorbed in my thoughts and awash with tears, and I prayed for the restoration of soul that only God can give.

My second loss was my friend Robert. The grief I faced at Robert's death was different from what I felt at Al's, for Robert was my contemporary. Robert was, as I had been, an executive in a Christian organization. He had all the external signs of health. One minute he was well and vital; the next minute he was diagnosed with MS that would take him away within four months. Death was the great intruder who not only took him away from me, but took him away at the peak of his creative and administrative powers.

I think that Robert's death affected me so deeply because I recognized afresh the *fragility* of life. I know that I had taught and preached on this theme countless times previously. But there was something about Robert's death in the middle of his years, his being struck down so quickly from the apparently impregnable heights of health and success, that I was left sad and wondering. I felt so bereft and isolated. *We are like a mist that arises in the morning and then vanishes*, I thought. *What, indeed, is the promise of life for any of us?*

That is exactly what I was wondering when my third friend died, just two weeks before I am writing this. Tom was a towering figure in the Christian world, a leader of African-American Christians and a powerful preacher of the gospel. Though he had been well known since his late twenties, only since his early forties had he established a rhythm and pace and commitment that satisfied him and maximized his many talents. I had heard him preach three months before his death, and he seemed fine. I did not know that he had leukemia, and that the form of it was not curable.

When he died, I cried out to God. I was overwhelmed with the *brevity* of life. *We are all like a vapor*, I thought, *a cloud that disappears*. "Oh, my God," I cried, "what is worth living for? Why should we expend so much time and so much effort in living and loving if the end result is that my friends die and many of them die prematurely? Why should *I* go on living? What should be the focus of my desire? My desires and longings don't diminish, but I can't seem to find anything compelling to which to direct them.

"I am tired, my God," I said, "tired of laboring and loving and losing and then having to do it all again and again. I am tired of the easy answers

I hear all around me, answers given by the TV and radio preachers who say that life is simple and all I need to do is follow several steps and I should be better. I am tired of the agony and the waste and the sense of injustice that I feel so deeply in my bones." I wondered for a fleeting moment why God had not chosen to take someone who really wanted to die, or someone whose death would not leave such a gaping hole in life as the hole left by my friends.

Life sometimes feels like my flesh is being torn from my bones. I feel some of that very deeply now. I think that my grief has made me able to understand Job's grief. I deeply believe that God is in the "restoration business," and I know that he really is shaping my life for his purposes. Sometimes the pain is so intense, but I believe that through it, God is gradually shaping the person that he wants me to be. I am finished with platitudes, but I still believe in the living God, the God who wounds me, but the One that also binds up the wounds.

Bill's Grief: Loss and Loneliness

Many years ago, when I was taking the Scholastic Aptitude Achievement Test in English composition, I was required to write an essay on a topic they provided. I still remember the statement they gave me. "Growing up requires the acceptance of limitations. Comment." That is all that it said. I had an hour to respond.

My first thought was of an exam that a philosophy professor once gave to his students, an exam consisting of only one question, "Why?" All the students flunked the exam except the two who responded, "Why not?" or "Because." I thought, for a fleeting moment, that I should respond similarly, perhaps with wry humor, "An hour provides too much of a *limitation* for such an *open-ended* statement."

Thankfully, my desire to get into a good college overrode my fledgling attempts at humor, and I developed a well-argued essay. I even remember the three points I made. I said that I agreed with the statement, and then I described the limitations that age brings: (1) acquisition of knowledge, (2) choice of a life partner and (3) focus on a field or profession. The point that I made was that in growing up our focus tends to narrow and that most of us will make our mark in the world *because* our focus narrows. Meaning and love are enhanced by the selection of one partner or the choice of one field. Growing up, I maintained, means that we need to leave many things behind.

As I grew older I recognized the truth of my essay. Limitations of all kinds began to face me. But in general I handled the limitations gracefully. Though sidelined by a football injury, I could participate in other sports, and even if they were not competitive sports at least they were fitness sports. I could not read *every* book in the university library; perhaps I could find a few that spoke powerfully to me. Limitations were part of the process of growing older.

Yet as year succeeded year and season followed season, I began to look at limitations in a different way. What had at first seemed simply to be limitations now seemed to be *losses*. What had been things that I accepted rather easily now became *lingering griefs*. What had been toys or lesser things that were put away so that I could take on the responsibilities of adulthood now appeared to be confirmations of mortality and indications that I was nearing my own death. Instead of being hopeful and optimistic about the future, I began to be dogged by grief and tears. It did not happen overnight. There were not really any warning signals that I can easily point to today. I was not overwhelmed by a tidal wave of sudden losses. It was more like having a quantity of sand in my hand which gradually seeped out as I tried to squeeze it tighter.

I vividly remember one experience that sums up the grief I felt. For years I had lived and worked hard in Portland, Oregon, and had after several years been able to find on any given working day someone that I knew on every city block. I remember going from greeting to greeting in the genial and optimistic days of the mid-1980s. Several years later, after I had left that city, I returned and walked its streets one summer afternoon. Though the streets and buildings were all familiar, I didn't see *anyone* I knew. I combed familiar blocks of downtown. I went by familiar restaurants. I even looked inside the places of particular significance for me in the past, hoping perhaps to see someone who had been so vital in those days. I stood for several minutes near the downtown square. Nothing. I knew no one. People walked past individually and in groups, carrying their burdens and joys, in light and serious converse, all oblivious to me.

The sense of loneliness and emptiness I experienced at that moment was overpowering. I felt that I had lost almost everything of value in my life. I did not begrudge anyone around me the happiness and joviality they were experiencing. Nor did I want to try to become part of the scene that I witnessed. I just felt for one aching moment that the conversation was going on without me and that if it could do so in places that were *so* familiar, then life could certainly continue very well without me.

One tear and then many coursed down my cheeks, and I escaped to the hills and familiar parks overlooking the city. I walked paths I had taken dozens of times before; I saw familiar trees and bends in the trail. I felt the same cool breeze and saw the same dank tufted moss sprouting from the ground and hanging from the bushes. Nature, it seemed, was welcoming me even if people did not. I remember calling on God and confessing my sense of loss, confusion and grief. I remember also that the feeling of grief simply did not go away. It kept burdening my heart, eating away at my satisfaction of being back "home," tearing at the inner recesses of my life.

I began to see that grief was a very real part of my life, a part that could, years ago, be interpreted simply as a limitation or a necessary loss, but now could not be so easily explained. I began to see that grief would accompany me for a while on my journey of life. I began to see grief as something like scar tissue, which actually covers a wound but is a constant reminder of that wound. Scar tissue serves a function, to be sure, but it also can endanger life. I have known people who have had to undergo serious heart bypass surgery because of a buildup of scar tissue from a previous surgery. I began to wonder whether the scar tissue of my grief might also endanger my life.

Other Griefs

I started to become sympathetic to the various ways in which grief is a part of all of our lives. Though this may not be a complete catalog of the reasons for grief, I think that we mourn today for three reasons: (1) the loss of one dear to us, (2) the loss or apparent loss of our dreams and (3) regrets about decisions or paths we have taken.

I, Bill, am thinking of a family that used to live just two doors from us. Tom was a prominent physician in town, and Stephanie was a visible community volunteer. Their three children were a source of delight to the family and neighborhood. Several years ago they moved to the country so that they could have horses and more room for gardens and crops. Even before they moved, some friends had begun to comment that Stephanie seemed to have a drinking problem. The problem worsened when they moved. The country provided loneliness and isolation rather than freedom from limitations. After three years her condition required extensive hospitalization. Friends said that they felt helpless as they prayed, confronted, conversed and ultimately realized that their efforts were of no avail.

Finally Stephanie, only in her mid-forties, died. The outpouring of grief and sadness shook the entire community. The gloom on the street was palpable. A friend was lost. It was, and is, so sad. The pain of the loss has not gone away.

Grief as a result of divorce or separation is a more frequent pain in our society. Though almost all couples who marry hope and expect that the union will last until one of them dies, the sad reality is that nearly 50 percent of all marriages in America end in divorce. The financial and emotional costs of divorce are enormous. Some have even said that the grief resulting from divorce is worse than from death, because in divorce someone has *chosen* to reject you. It is impossible to understand the growth of the counseling movement, both secular and Christian, in our society in the 1980s without understanding how it is "married" to the prevalence of divorce or separation in our culture.

Grief is also caused by lost dreams, a point we will examine below as we describe the stages of Job's grief.

Finally, grief is caused by regrets. We all instinctively understand the hero who has some regrets. In a scene in the film *Chariots of Fire*, Scotsman Eric Liddell refused to run his qualifying heat for the one-hundred-meter dash in the 1924 Olympics on a Sunday. When this took him out of the competition for the gold medal in that event, he was asked whether he had any regrets. His terse response was, "Regrets, yes, but no doubts." As it happened, other opportunities for Liddell to run developed, and he ended up winning the four-hundred-meter dash.

Yet sometimes our regrets are not so easily put aside. Not long ago I was speaking with a prominent president of a Christian college. He had a long and illustrious career as a leader in higher education. We spoke together easily about his past and about significant individuals whom he felt had shaped him. But then, in a moment of hesitation, he mentioned to me that he was still working so hard at his age (around seventy) because he regretted a decision he made more than thirty years ago to enter college administration. If he had his life to live over again, he said, he would have stayed in the classroom, kept abreast of scholarly developments in his field, written a lot more and spent less time at fund-raising dinners. Regrets come in all shapes and sizes, and a person's position in life gives no assurance that he or she is not burdened with the grief of unmet longings.

We usually think of grief as something that individuals or families share, but grief is also a larger phenomenon, involving groups or even nations. Not long ago, I visited a pastor friend of mine who had for several years been active in denominational affairs. Though I knew that there was considerable controversy in the denomination regarding how liberals and conservatives were going to live together in the future, I was not ready for her comments about the future of the church. She told me in passionate, clipped sentences that something was very wrong in the church as she saw it, that it was like a death was taking place, and that people at the national level were grieving over the present and future of the church.

I also saw grief on a larger scale when I visited Israel recently. The grief was most pronounced in the Gaza Strip, a 140-square-mile section of land (inhabited by more than 800,000 people) which received autonomy from Israel in May 1994. I talked about the future of the Gaza Strip with a young lawyer, winner of the Robert F. Kennedy Award for Human Rights in 1991. So overwhelmed was he by the realities of the situation, including the lack of good water, the hundreds of thousands of refugees living in horrendous conditions, the rampant unemployment, the increasing hopelessness and the continued humiliations at the hands of the Israelis that he simply could not speak. Every question I raised was met with a troubled, brief or incoherent response. His silence was the silence of grief, grief not simply for himself but for a people who have lived under occupation for many years and who do not know which way to turn. Grief, individual or corporate, is a pressing and oppressing reality for us today.

Whether we will ever be able to put our grief behind us is not easy to say. Most people who have experienced devastating loss, especially the loss of a child or a spouse, would say that they will never get over the sense of emptiness and loneliness which the absence has brought. Yet the Scriptures teach us that pain, loneliness and grief are not the bottom line or the last word in life. By hearing the Scriptures speak of grief and show us grief, we are better able to understand our own grief and perhaps discover a new life that will emerge through the grief. We know that one day, in the heavenly kingdom, all weeping will be over. Maybe, just maybe, by the grace of God and our own diligent study and living, not all of us will have to wait until that time for our mourning to stop.

Happiness and Heartbreak: Two Scripture Stories

One comforting fact about the Scriptures is that they provide us insight and company for any human emotion or action. Even though we might tend to become lost in our private griefs, we ought to realize that the Bible tells us stories of others in similar circumstances and these stories not only can comfort, they can instruct and guide us.

While Job is the biblical person most well known for his grievous trials, two others stand out as well—Hannah and David.

Hannah, wife of Elkanah, was a loyal follower of Yahweh, but she was could not bear children (1 Samuel 1). Barrenness in ancient Israel was a social embarrassment as well as sign of divine disapproval. Without children one's lineage stopped. Without children you had no "afterlife." Taking her grief to the tabernacle of God in Shiloh, Hannah poured out her soul. "In bitterness of soul Hannah wept much and prayed to the LORD" (1 Samuel 1:10). In her grief she *bargained* with God (a term we will meet below), and promised to dedicate her son to God's service if he allowed her to become pregnant. Eli, the priest, heard her bitter and incoherent praying and thought she was drunk. But Hannah stood her ground and told of her vow to God. Her faithfulness and great anguish and grief touched the heart of God, and she bore a son, whom she named Samuel. This baby—a future great spiritual leader—was indeed a happy outcome to a bitter grief.

David, king of Israel, was not so fortunate. Though his son Absalom led a palace revolt against David, David still doted on him. In no uncertain terms David told his military people that if Absalom was apprehended, he should be brought back safely. But as war and luck would have it, Absalom was run through by Joab, David's military commander (2 Samuel 18:14). When David heard the news, he became inconsolable. He said, "O my son Absalom! My son, my son Absalom! If only I had died instead of you—O Absalom, my son, my son!" (2 Samuel 18:33). Even on his deathbed, David wanted revenge on Joab for his violent behavior—"Now you yourself know what Joab son of Zeruiah did to me. . . . Deal with him according to your wisdom, but do not let his gray head go down to the grave in peace" (1 Kings 2:5-6). The grief of David's loss, coupled with his inability to forget or forgive, accompanied him to the grave.

Job and the Stages of Grief
Obviously it will not be easy or automatic to get beyond our grief. But there may be things we can learn from Job's grief that will help us un-

derstand our own and move, by God's grace, to a position where it does not dominate our lives. Let us turn to the story of Job again, and examine the nature of Job's grief.

Job's loss, as we have seen, was massive and sudden. All was well with him, he says (16:12), and then the troubles began. Once they started, they continued in rapid, staccato fashion until he had lost almost everything he prized: children, wealth, home and health. His wife still survived, but she counseled Job to "curse God and die" (2:9), probably thinking that Job's death would be better for him than continued living. As the book unfolds, the reader is confronted with the terrifying possibility that Job also has lost or will lose his friends and his God. Loss characterizes Job's situation: sudden, violent, complete and devastating. Unlike many of us who have warnings when disasters come, he had no time to prepare in any way for the divine storm that tore through his life.

As I have tried to understand Job's grief, I have found Elisabeth Kübler-Ross's now-classic presentation of the stages of grief very helpful. My goal here is to describe briefly her approach to grief and then show how Job's experience reflects but also goes beyond Kübler-Ross's description.

Kübler-Ross's theory arises from numerous interviews she and others conducted with terminally ill cancer patients in Chicago in the late 1960s. Her 1969 work *On Death and Dying*, revolutionary at the time, was based on the premise that the dying have a lot to teach the living, that the lessons of those facing *death* might teach us better how to face *life*. In the course of the interviews she began to recognize that the sufferings of people, though unique and individual, were expressed in certain patterns or stages as the person grew closer and closer to death.

The five stages of grief she isolated were denial, anger, bargaining, depression and acceptance.

Denial. At first, when patients learned that they had a terminal disease, their typical response was, "No, not me, it cannot be true" (p. 38). In most cases this stage lasted only a short time. It was absolutely critical for people to get beyond denial if they were to move on to other stages of grief, stages which Kübler-Ross considered helpful for both the patient and his or her family.

Anger. Next, the sense that their life had been interrupted and the realization that they had new limitations usually made people angry. They were no longer free to determine their comings and goings; they were subject to others' plans for everything from eating to sleeping to taking medicine. So the person would usually cry out. Anger would be directed against anyone and anything: doctors prescribing the treatment, nurses providing the care, spouses just becoming used to this new routine, the patient's new diet, the room's decor, the lighting, the bed. Anger was always a reflection of something deeper, of the loss of control and of the sense that people were already considering him or her dead.

Bargaining. The third stage, which Kübler-Ross calls bargaining, consists of the patient's resolve to make a deal with God. *Perhaps,* thinks the person, *God will postpone or alleviate the more negative aspects of my illness if I am nice rather than angry.* So the person makes a deal with God. We have already seen an interesting example of this in Hannah's prayer to God about a son. Perhaps she was barren because God was angry in some way; if she bargained with God by promising that her son would go into divine service, maybe, just maybe, God would reward her with a son.

Depression. The fourth stage of grief results from the fact that the terminal nature of the illness has finally sunk in. There is no escape; there will be no reversal. Coupled with the realization of the finality of the condition is the weight of other burdens: *Who will care for the things that were my responsibility? How will people deal with the financial strain I have caused? How will I be remembered?* It all seems too much, and the person may descend into despair.

Acceptance. Finally, Kübler-Ross speaks of a stage when the person is neither happy nor sad; rather, he or she is almost devoid of feelings. It is as if the pain is gone and the struggle is over, as if the battle has already been fought. As one patient phrased it, at this time she needs "the final rest before the long journey" (p. 113). Usually the person sits in silence, though he or she may desire human contact.

Much research on death and dying has been done since Kübler-Ross's groundbreaking book. There has been a lot of discussion about the particular stages she identifies and whether one can break down the experience of dying as neatly as she seems to suggest. Many would claim, and the experience of Job confirms, that the stages seem to run together and separate, much like streams that merge and separate after a heavy rain. Anger and depression may alternate, as night follows day and day follows night.

I would say that Job went through at least four stages of grief: denial, anger, depression or resignation, and defiance. Three of these are similar to Kübler-Ross's characterization, but the fourth, defiance, is unexpected; perhaps it is this man's attitude of defiance that gives the book of Job its peculiar power. Job is a person who not only feels melancholy and pervasive sadness but also possesses a streak of stubborn durability, resilience and outright audacity. Job's ability to fly from resigned hopelessness to defiant audacity is perhaps the key to understanding the depth of his grief.

Sinking in Dishonor and Despair

Few Scripture verses are more hopeless than those that come from Job's mouth. Listen to a few of them:

What strength do I have, that I should still hope?

What prospects, that I should be patient? (6:11)

My days are swifter than a weaver's shuttle,

and they come to an end without hope. (7:6)

As water wears away stones

and torrents wash away the soil,

so you destroy man's hope. (14:19)

Note that in the last verse Job attributes his loss of hope to God. Though God *could* heap blessings upon us, for some inexplicable reason he sometimes chooses to wreak havoc in our lives.

Without hope, Job sees no purpose in living:

I loathe my very life;

therefore I will give free rein to my complaint

and speak out in the bitterness of my soul. (10:1)
I despise my life; I would not live forever.
   Let me alone; my days have no meaning. (7:16)
Although I am blameless,
   I have no concern for myself;
   I despise my own life. (9:21)

The depth of Job's despair and grief makes him believe that his life, which was once such a rich, honored and meaningful life, is irretrievably over.

   Remember, O God, that my life is but a breath;
   my eyes will never see happiness again. (7:7)
My spirit is broken,
   my days are cut short,
   the grave awaits me. (17:1)
My days have passed, my plans are shattered,
   and so are the desires of my heart. (17:11)

What is particularly wrenching for Job is that his distress has not only left him childless, poor and unhealthy but also *dishonored* him. In Middle Eastern cultures honor goes a long way. When I was in Saudi Arabia in 1993, I noticed that our Saudi host would greet friends as we went through the streets of Jedda or Riyadh and that the greetings would last perhaps three or four minutes. After witnessing this time after time, I took our host aside and asked about the Saudi greeting. He said that it took so long to greet another person, even if you had seen him rather recently, because you had to heap up phrases that were worthy of the other person's honor. You had to ransack the lexicon, as it were, to find terms that were exalted enough to match the honor of your friend. Some of the phrases we might consider amusing, such as "Greetings to the finest man in town! To the most distinguished son of the area! To the one whose dignity and honor and children bring blessing to the entire nation!" But they were essential to preserving the highly honed Middle Eastern sense of honor. Words of honor preserve the society. They reinforce each person's position and indispensability in that society.

   When Job was devastated, then, he suffered a consequent diminution

of his honor, and a lessening of his honor meant that Job himself was less
of a person. Job knows this and laments it. Hear his plaintive cry:

> He has alienated my brothers from me;
>> my acquaintances are completely estranged from me.
> My kinsmen have gone away;
>> my friends have forgotten me.
> My guests and my maidservants count me a stranger;
>> they look upon me as an alien.
> I summon my servant, but he does not answer,
>> though I beg him with my own mouth.
> My breath is offensive to my wife;
>> I am loathsome to my own brothers.
> Even the little boys scorn me;
>> when I appear, they ridicule me.
> All my intimate friends detest me;
>> those I love have turned against me. (19:13-19)

Job's sense of loss, fueled by his familial, fiscal and bodily loss, is well
captured in the greeting he now receives:

> But now they mock me,
>> men younger than I,
> whose fathers I would have disdained
>> to put with my sheep dogs. (30:1)

The whole structure of Job's finely crafted world has come crashing down
around him. All the king's horses and all the king's men are no match for
the tumultuous and total devastation of Job.

Rising Up in Holy Boldness

But rather surprisingly, Job does not give up. His head is bloodied but
unbowed. He gathers strength from somewhere deep within the reser-
voirs of his being, and makes his appeal to God. His attitude is captured
in 10:1, a verse I have quoted above:

> I loathe my very life;
>> therefore I will give free rein to my complaint

and speak out in the bitterness of my soul.

Job is saying, in essence, "Well, my life is over. I hate it. God has done all this to me. So, what do I have to lose? Why not say exactly what is on my mind? What is God going to do, *punish* me?"

It is reasoning like this that contributes to Job's audacity, or what I call his holy boldness. We are familiar with this phenomenon in other areas of human life. Often a person who has come face to face with death and has lived to tell it, now has a completely different attitude toward *life*. Every day is special, full of opportunities which one should face without fear, overflowing with possibilities for life. Once you have nearly given up your life, the thought of giving it up again is not so daunting.

So Job will speak in the bitterness of his spirit. He has nothing to lose. He may die soon, but he has silently resolved that he will not go "gentle into that good night." Rather, in the words of Dylan Thomas, he will "rage against the dying of the light." His grief is leading him on; his resiliency and suppleness require him to approach God again. Hear his words:

If only I knew where to find him;
    if only I could go to his dwelling!
I would state my case before him
    and fill my mouth with arguments.
I would find out what he would answer me,
    and consider what he would say.
Would he oppose me with great power?
    No, he would not press charges against me.
There an upright man could present his case before him,
    and I would be delivered forever from my judge. . . .
When he has tested me, I will come forth as gold. (23:3-7, 10)

Job's confidence is growing even as his human comforters are fading.

Yet I am not silenced by the darkness,
    by the thick darkness that covers my face. (23:17)

Even though God is inaccessible and may still be angry, Job feels that he has right on his side. Christians today have a slogan: "God plus one makes a majority." Job would have had a slightly different slogan: "Justice plus one makes a majority, even over against God." Job wants his case to be recorded and written on a scroll; better yet he wants it inscribed "in rock forever" (19:23-24).

So confident is Job of his eventual victory that as he signs his defense, he urges God to put *his* indictment in writing. What would Job do with this divine indictment?

Surely I would wear it on my shoulder,
I would put it on like a crown. . . .
like a prince I would approach him. (31:36-37)

Job would be *proud* of the divine indictment and would wear it as a badge of distinction so that all could see. This reminds me of a conversation I had with a young Palestinian student in May 1994 at Bir Zeit University in the occupied West Bank. We were speaking about his political involvement, and I asked whether he had ever been arrested by the Israelis. "Of course," he responded. Then he looked around the cafeteria and with a sweep of his hand said, "About 70 percent of the people in this cafeteria have been arrested or detained since the beginning of the Intifada" (in December 1987).

I, a law-abiding American, asked him how he and his compatriots felt about that. His response was illuminating. "It is like a badge of honor, a sign that you are involved actively in the struggle, that you haven't given up your hope or your future. We are proud of having been arrested for our beliefs."

It is this same confidence, this reckless audacity, this unbending stubbornness, this chronic insubordination, this unyielding chutzpah, that Job possesses. His grief is real, very real, and he expresses his hopelessness too often for it to be overlooked or ignored. Yet a strange and strong spunkiness also characterizes Job. He has nothing to lose. He feels that he is in the right. He will approach God. And then he will wait for God's response. What else, really, can he do?

Learning from Job's Grief

We may not feel that we suffer exactly as Job suffered. Some of us seem willing to live quietly with our grief and pain, as wounded animals sometimes do. Yet Job teaches us some things about grief that we ought not ignore.

The first lesson about grief is that we need to express it. Shakespeare, our incomparable bard, captures the sentiment exactly in *Macbeth* (act 4, scene 3):

Give sorrow words. The grief that does not speak
Whispers the o'er-fraught heart, and bids it break.

We may feel that we would break if we express our grief; Shakespeare's words teach the opposite. We might break if we *don't* tell our grief. By speaking of it we contribute to that great and unending song of pain and redemption, taught us by our Creator and directed by the Son of God. Holding the pain in only increases it, as the prophet Jeremiah knew when he tried to hold the Word of God within him:

But if I say, "I will not mention him
    or speak any more in his name,"
his word is in my heart like a fire,
    a fire shut up in my bones.
I am weary of holding it in;
    indeed, I cannot. (Jeremiah 20:9)

Grief contained will eventually break the container; grief flowing freely, like the tears that flow down our cheeks, is grief that can be healed.

A second lesson Job teaches us is that grief changes us. I have friends who refer to the two stages of their married life as "B.K." and "A.K.," meaning, of course, "before and after kids." Why? Because as every parent knows, the presence of children changes you in almost every way, from the privacy you once had in the middle of the night and on weekends to the plans that you must make to accommodate more people in the car, the restaurant and the playroom.

So it is with grief. Diane Cole has written a fine book on grieving and losing, entitled *After Great Pain a New Life Emerges.* Her major point is that grief, when it came on her and her family and friends, not only devastated them but, inevitably, changed them. After grief the spring of your step is not quite so springy; the laugh is not quite so carefree or frequent; the range of jokes is not quite as broad as before.

Grief can also deepen people, coloring their Christian character as nothing else can. Paul, in the letter to the Philippians, states that the goal of his Christian life is to know Christ and the "fellowship of sharing in his sufferings" (Philippians 3:10). Those who share in grief form a special fellowship that can *identify and identify with* each other in ways that people who have not suffered cannot imagine. Those who have grieved are those who have been changed and deepened. Instead of a beloved child, bereaved parents may have to settle for understanding and wisdom and new relationships that they never would have chosen. Grief changes and deepens us.

But we need to take care lest grief also harden us. Grief may make us insensible to the sufferings of others because of the mountain of our own grief. Grief may take away compassion from our hearts because we feel that compassion no longer exists in the core of the universe. Grief may reduce us to a brittleness that *looks* like hardness but is ready to crack at the application of the slightest pressure, like the ribbon candy that I used to sell as a Cub Scout more than thirty-five years ago.

Therefore, we need to expect that God will not leave us unanswered in our grief. Grief may persist and continue to be our companion, long after we hoped that we were healed and ready to return to normal life. But what Job would tell us is that his grief, when he expressed it honestly to God, with his wild hopes and utter hopelessness, was finally addressed by God. Grief just doesn't go away; time doesn't naturally heal all wounds. Only God can bring a touch of healing and understanding to the griefs that fill our lives and dominate our thoughts. God will speak, as Job attests, to the weary and worn out of heart. God speaks to those who try. God speaks to those who are genuine and straightforward and earnest in their grief. Our God, discovered Job, is not for the faint at heart; our God can take whatever we can throw at him. God wants us to "give him our best" not simply in seeking success or cultivating relationships but also in expressing our griefs. You will find as Job discovered, that a new world waits for you on the other side of your griefs.

Prayer

O sovereign God, the author and finisher of history and of my life, I and my friends and family grieve today. I have been given so much, but sometimes all I can think about is what I *lack* or have lost. I try to remain grateful for life, but then thoughts of pains and griefs so fill my mind that I can think of nothing else. I need to be able to understand and get control of my griefs, but they really are running my life. I am scared so often, God. I am afraid of what might develop with my body, with the friction that is between people, with the hopelessness that meets me and others so often. Forgive me for my willingness to give in to the griefs that surround me. Give me some of Job's spunkiness and confidence and boldness before you. Deepen me through the griefs, that I may be able to touch the lives of others with the precious news of your love. Through Jesus Christ our Lord, amen.

Questions for Study and Discussion

1. What griefs do people in your immediate world face? With what words or actions do they express their griefs?

2. What griefs do you bear? Did they wash over you suddenly, like a tidal wave, or creep up on you, like a stealthy intruder?

3. How do you feel about expressing your honest griefs to God, even if the language and thoughts that you use are out of character for you?

4. If you could change one thing in your life that brings or has brought you grief, what would that be?

5. In your judgment, can griefs be healed? Or must we always wear them, much like a disfiguring scar or a stain that simply will not come out?

JOB 19:1-2
Then Job replied:
"How long will you torment me
    and crush me with words?"

6

FRIEND
TO FRIEND

I n many ways, we, Glandion and Bill, should have never become friends, much less coauthors. We live in a time of polarized race relations in our country, and Glandion is African-American and Bill is Caucasian. We are far different from each other; Glandion is a man of immense spiritual sensitivity and discernment, while Bill is a person with finely honed organizational and planning skills. Glandion has been a pastor; Bill, a professor. Glandion is geared toward the feel of a text; Bill is analytically oriented. When one of our mutual friends heard that we were going to write a book together, much less a series of books, he exclaimed, "It just can't be!"

We are both men in our early or mid-forties and had met each other briefly in California around 1970. We didn't meet again until the fall of 1990, when Glandion was the spiritual-emphasis week speaker at Sterling College in Kansas, where Bill had just begun to teach history and government. We were socially polite to each other over a group lunch and in a personal conversation. Then something began to click between us. Though one can never pinpoint the precise moment when a friendship begins, I believe it came through two things—a dawning realization and a personal openness.

We came to realize that it was pretty unusual for our paths to cross in a rural Kansas town twenty years after they had crossed in a major American city. We looked at each other and saw that *neither* of us was a rural person (our backgrounds were urban and suburban), *neither* of us knew our way around the institution that supported us, and *neither* of us, frankly, could tell the other very convincingly why he was here. Why were we here in Sterling, Kansas? We began to see it as God's sovereign and even humorous way of guiding our lives. Perhaps God was guiding us together for something whose contours and scope we could scarcely imagine.

The second thing that enabled a friendship to develop was our *availability*. Availability is more than just having free time or being able and willing to speak with someone. *Availability*, as I use the word, means that you anticipate and even yearn for meaning and relationships. Availability is an attitude of life, an orientation or stance toward the world, that looks for opportunities to say yes to life. We were available to each other.

So many of us, I believe, have already sealed off large segments of our life from the possibility of meaning or joy that we are closed to the possibilities that God may be spreading out right in front of us. Many of us have been hurt before in a relationship, so we have quietly resolved in the recesses of our mind that in order to avoid being hurt again, we will no longer be available to anyone. Many of us feel like we have failed, so we will not try again. Many of us feel that a "no" whispered by someone else on one occasion long ago is a definitive and binding and irreversible no—one that still screams at us and will scream at us for the rest of our lives. It is just too painful to think about trying again.

Life belongs, we are convinced, to those who still give life a chance. Faith belongs to those who believe that God is not finished with them yet. But even if you say yes to life and to each other, if you are available for another, that doesn't mean that the road you will travel together will be easy or always neat and rewarding. We, Glandion and Bill, have seen each other when times were not good—for example, when Bill was considering dropping the project on the Psalms *(Longing for God)* because of personal doubts (what good will *another* book on the Psalms do anyone?) or when Glandion was devastated by the loss of three dear friends within a year. We have been short with one another or unable to get back to one another when we should have done so.

But that is the bad stuff! Whenever we talk, we easily pick up where we last broke off. We celebrate each other's moves and family joys, we share our personal fears and hopes, we carve out a sacred space that only we are privileged to enter. Our words feed each other as dry tinder feeds a blazing fire, and our questions, yearnings and thoughts are shared with openness, freedom and receptivity. We don't try to impress each other; we don't need to try to fool each other; there really is no need to be anything but honest with each other. We do not feel that our friendship is meant to prove anything to anybody, but we are gradually thinking that this unique relationship may have meaning and hold encouragement for others beyond us, others who would like to build bridges between the races and between different sorts of people.

Keys for Friendship

We could list several characteristics of friends and friendship, but the two most important in our opinion are that *friends don't judge each other* and that *friends don't feel that they have to "fix" each other.* Friends give each other space to say and do what the other needs. Nineteenth-century English author George Eliot expresses it perfectly:

Oh the comfort, the inexpressible comfort of feeling safe with a person: having neither to weigh thoughts nor measure words, but to pour them out. Just as they are—chaff and grain together, knowing that a faithful hand will take and sift them, keep what is worth keeping, and then with the breath of kindness, blow the rest away.

A friend is one who can hear my deep things without condescension or manipulation, without the need to make me feel good or bad or anything. A friend is one who listens to me and receives the struggle I tell as an authentic struggle, as a battle with real beasts and enemies and with mortal danger to me if I do not escape. A friend is one who hears me.

One of the only places in the Psalms where the psalmist says that he loves the Lord is when he knows he has been heard:

I love the LORD, for he heard my voice;

he heard my cry for mercy.

Because he turned his ear to me,

I will call on him as long as I live. (Psalm 116:1-2)

God, in this passage, is the true friend, the one who has heard us and responded to us according to our deepest needs.

But a true friend is also one who doesn't feel the need to "fix" us or to "solve" our problems in order to remain a friend. I know that one of my biggest fears long ago, before friendship played an important role for me, was that if I developed a serious relationship with a person and they asked me for help, *I might not be able to provide it!* That is, my greatest anxiety was that I might not know how to help a person in an area that they had not even specified to me. It was like never wanting to get a car because I might not know what to do if it should develop a problem!

I think that I was unconsciously reflecting a very American approach to relationships, an approach that characterizes relationships among Christians too. Relationships, I felt, were like story problems in math. You have a problem and you have to come up with a solution, and sometimes you get the wrong answer. But the goal of relationships, as of math problems, was to get the right answer or to "solve the problem." I saw friendship as a chance to give people advice and suggestions on how to make their life better.

I was, unconsciously, also using a medical model in dealing with my friends. Thomas Moore, in his recent book *Soul Mates*, points out how characteristic it is for Americans to look at relationships and problems as something to be "healed" rather than something to be "lived with" or to "learn from." I know that I was hoping to straighten up people's lives and return them to the joy of the gospel.

As I thought further about friendships and my need to "fix" people, or make them better, I saw that this need of mine rested on another belief I had, a belief so deeply embedded in my consciousness that even today I have a hard time getting rid of it. It is the belief that we ought not to live in a messy world, and that somehow, if we really were spiritual people, things would not be as messy as they were. If we really were committed Christians, I believed, life simply would not be so complicated, difficult and unseemly. Therefore, I had the unconscious need to try to remove the messiness from people's lives so that their life and mine would be a closer approximation of what I thought a good world should be. I failed to see at that time that the world has an inherent chaos and disorder to it. Some might attribute this to original sin, some to the press of so many people trying to eke out a living on such a small planet, some to the particular whims and demands of demanding people. Part of the wonder of the world is precisely its unpredictability, its seeming inability or unwillingness to conform to rules, human or divine, as it continues to develop.

I then began to see that the key to friendship is not to fix someone but to be honest with them, not to solve their problems but to invest in them, not to clean up their mess but to offer a connection that demonstrates trust and commitment to another person. Friendship is a process of engaging with another person at any place or time, of walking with them as far along the valley as we and they can go together, of singing and rejoicing with them even when we don't really know the tune and are not quite sure why we are singing the song. We are made for friendships as we are made for God—our hearts are restless until they find their rest in both. William Blake, that strange and wonderful English poet of two hundred years ago, said it best and briefest: "The bird a nest, the spider a web, man friendship."

Job and His Friends
As we study the conversation between Job and his friends, we are not looking to convict the friends of lack of sensitivity or Job of having a quick tongue. We would like to hear how they speak, for their speech gives us

an indication of their relationship to Job and how they think of Job's distress. We would also like to understand what makes the conversation work and how it "breaks down." Finally, we would like to discover whether there are lessons that Job can teach us about friendship and conversation today.

Let us start *before* conversation, for that is where the acts of friendship begin. We read in Job 2:

> When Job's three friends, Eliphaz the Temanite, Bildad the Shuhite and Zophar the Naamathite, heard about all the troubles that had come upon him, they set out from their homes and met together by agreement to go and sympathize with him and comfort him. When they saw him from a distance, they could hardly recognize him; they began to weep aloud, and they tore their robes and sprinkled dust on their heads. Then they sat on the ground with him for seven days and seven nights. No one said a word to him, because they saw how great his suffering was. (Job 2:11-13)

The friends were friends, in the first instance, because they *went* to him, they *wept* with him and they *waited* with him. They set out to comfort Job in whatever way they could. They followed the custom of Middle Eastern hospitality and commiseration by not speaking until the host and sufferer had first spoken. The period of silence lasted an entire week, and it must have tested the resolve and friendship of the three. After all, since they were friends of Job, they also were probably wealthy and influential people. As we know from our own day, this kind of people often does not have a week to spare just to sit on the ground in torn clothes with someone. They are rich precisely because they have spent their time efficiently, by cutting deals, making decisions and paying attention to the big and small details of work. They have now sacrificed to be with Job in his distress. They are open to him and waiting to respond to his needs.

But what are their obligations as friends, according to the worldview of the time? The clearest verse from wisdom literature (of which the book of Job is a part) that lays out the duties of friends is Proverbs 17:17:

> A friend loves at all times,

and a brother is born for adversity.

Friends are present with one another—especially in times of trouble. The friends must also have been aware that it was in times of need, rather than prosperity, where friendship shows its true colors. The ancient book of Ecclesiasticus teaches the same, "A friend cannot be known in prosperity" (12:8). They would also have known the truth of the terse saying from Proverbs 18:

A man of many companions may come to ruin,

but there is a friend who sticks closer than a brother. (v. 24)

No doubt *they* intended to be that friend, the one who sticks closer than a brother, the one who was there for their friend Job in his moment of deepest need. Their intentions were matched by their actions.

Finally, they knew there was an additional duty incumbent on friends, a duty which was a hard one for them, a duty that might be misunderstood and might be misperformed, but an essential duty of friendship. Put briefly, it was to tell each other the truth, even if it hurt. Proverbs says the following:

Faithful are the wounds of a friend;

profuse are the kisses of an enemy. (Proverbs 27:6 RSV)

That is, the process of counseling or comforting a friend may lead to injury. A surgeon may have to reopen a wound and start the bleeding again in order to heal a person from the wound. A hurt may need to be hurt again before healing takes place. So the friends knew that one of the painful duties of friendship was to wound, if necessary, so that Job could be healed. Let us examine briefly how each of the three spoke to Job.

Eliphaz the Temanite

Presumably the oldest of the three, Eliphaz speaks in Job 4—5, 15 and 22. The main lines of his approach to Job and his problem are evident in Job 4—5 and Job 15. His approach is *gentle* and *affirmative* at first and then becomes *firm*. Like Bildad and Zophar, he believes in the view of life that says when suffering comes your way, it is because either *you* have done something to deserve it or *God* is somehow testing your faithfulness.

129

Though he tries to remain understanding and compassionate, at times he says things at which a thoughtful person would take offense.

Eliphaz gently speaks to Job:

If someone ventures a word with you, will you be impatient?

But who can keep from speaking? (4:2)

Eliphaz sees the distress of his friend and wants to ease his way into the conversation. He will find, however, it is like easing into an icy swimming pool one inch at a time.

He ever so gently chides Job:

Your words have supported those who stumbled;

you have strengthened faltering knees.

But now trouble comes to you, and you are discouraged;

it strikes you, and you are dismayed. (4:4-5)

Eliphaz is quietly suggesting to Job that he, who has been a tower of strength to others when they were suffering, now needs to be that same tower when he suffers in his own life. "Take your own advice, Job," he says. "By complaining, you are running the risk of hurting others' faith."

But you even undermine piety

and hinder devotion to God. (15:4)

The main lines of Eliphaz's words to Job are these:

☐ *Words of comfort:* "Where were the upright ever destroyed?" (4:7). Eliphaz thinks that Job is upright and that he should therefore take comfort. These distresses are *not* meant to destroy Job.

☐ *Words of vision:* Eliphaz relates a night vision he had which revealed that all people are sinners (4:13-17).

☐ *Words of sober reality:* "Yet man is born to trouble as surely as sparks fly upward" (5:7).

☐ *Words of friendly advice:* "But if it were I, I would appeal to God; I would lay my cause before him" (5:8).

☐ *Words of hope:* In 5:17-27 Eliphaz tries to encourage Job by showing that the person whom God corrects (Job) is really a blessed person or a happy person. God wounds, but he also binds the wounds. God will deliver and will bring laughter to Job again.

Though Eliphaz has played the role of friend well, he still cannot hide some judgmental feelings. In his description of the fool he says, "His children are far from safety" (5:4). Might not Job hear some judgment on *his* children, who, like the fool's children, were far from safety? Eliphaz speaks of the "six calamities" from which God will rescue the person whom God corrects (5:19). Why, Job might think, didn't God rescue *me* from these calamities?

Words slip out from the mouths of friends, our friends, even if they are trying to be comforting. Deb, whose story I will tell in the next chapter, relates that when she had just lost her husband to brain cancer, a well-meaning but not well-thinking person said, "You are still young and attractive and will be able to marry again." Julie said that after her son Will was lost in an accident, a person tried to comfort her with the words, "Well, you can still become pregnant and have another child." It was almost as if friends were afraid to let Deb or Julie experience her pain and thus tried to provide remedies that were, at the point of loss, absolutely the furthest things from her mind.

Eliphaz then provided comfort, advice and not a few mixed signals through his words. He urged Job to take his case to God and lay his cause before him. This, ultimately, is the advice that Job will heed. Yet confusion begins to take over the conversation, since Eliphaz and Job will develop different expectations of Job's approach to God. Eliphaz thinks that Job ought to do this and then rest quietly in faith with the friends. Job ultimately does this because he considers his friends' advice worthless. Eliphaz and the friends say, "Go to God and stay with us." Job says, in effect, "I'll go to God because *you* are no help." Distance is already entering into the conversation.

Bildad and Zophar

Things take a turn for the worse when Bildad and Zophar speak. Again, however, we should avoid the temptation to blame them for this. Bildad and Zophar are friends with their own needs. They bring a distinctive flavor to the conversation that moves it along *and* hinders it. I will examine Bildad's words in Job 8 and Zophar's in Job 11.

Bildad is direct, challenging, hopeful and ambiguous. Whereas Eliphaz seems to adopt the "counselor as comforter" model, Bildad believes in the "counselor as confronter" approach. Don't *we* say we believe in tough love, the direct approach, the approach that cuts through all the fluff? Don't we sometimes need someone who confronts us directly with the problem? Even if such a person sometimes overstates the case, isn't this model based on the presumption that sometimes you need to "shake things up" in order to get them back in working order? Both Bildad and Zophar do this. In the words of a popular book of the last decade, they "care enough to confront."

Bildad confronts Job on the level of his belief in God and the events of his life. By complaining against God so vigorously, Job is attacking God.

Does God pervert justice?

Does the Almighty pervert what is right? (8:3)

Bildad won't let Job slip by with his dangerous and potentially blasphemous words about God (Job 6—7). Bildad believes that *right thought and right belief* are important in life, and that Job is swimming very close to dangerous shoals.

Bildad also confronts Job with his own loss. In words that sound cruel Bildad says,

When your children sinned against him,

he gave them over to the penalty of their sin. (8:4)

Whoa! Run that by me again! Bildad is stating quite baldly that Job's children got what was coming to them! The doctrine of retribution is so strongly embedded in Bildad's mind that all of life must fit into its mold. Bildad has no room for mystery, no opportunity for the inexplicable chaos that enters our lives. There is a simple reason: human sin.

Bildad is not trying to be difficult. He bases his position on long tradition (8:8-19) which says that there are rules to the universe and that if the rules are broken, there are consequences. As a youth minister once said to me, "You don't break God's rules; they break you." So Bildad appeals to the ancients:

Ask the former generations
and find out what their fathers learned,
for we were born only yesterday and know nothing,
and our days on earth are but a shadow. (8:8-9)

The lesson that the ancient people teach us is that people who forget God perish. They may flourish for a while, like a well-watered plant in sunshine, but they will soon be uprooted from their place.

Such a condition may or may not be Job's, according to Bildad. He *seems* to say that Job is in danger; he *hopes* that God will "yet fill your mouth with laughter and your lips with shouts of joy" (8:21). The principle is clear—God does not reject a blameless person—but whether Job is blameless or not, well, the jury is still out.

Bildad is certainly in the grip of his own beliefs, but, to be fair, those beliefs are the same as Job's! Job is now questioning his beliefs, but he has not changed them. The reason for Job's torment is that he can't give up either his belief or his experience. Bildad thinks, then, that the best thing he can do for his friend is to go directly to the point, to confront him with the facts as he sees them, and then to hold out the possibility of hope.

What we see in Bildad is not too different from what we see in friends today; his sort of directness can put us off. But Bildad is trying, in his mind, to win back an erring brother to the fold. Sometimes gentleness is helpful, and Eliphaz has supplied that. Other times require a stricter regimen, which may indeed backfire, but which also may "shock" a person back to reality and life. Such a friend is Bildad.

If Bildad is confrontative, while still holding out hope, Zophar is judgmental and mean. He is bothered by Job's protestations of innocence. He is enraged by Job's inability to see his situation rationally. He hopes that God would speak and straighten him out, but since God seems reluctant to do this, Zophar jumps into the gap and fills the silence of God. Zophar believes, like Bildad and Eliphaz, that life works according to laws or rules. The central rule of life is that the wicked perish and the righteous are rewarded in this life. It is a tried and true doctrine. Its truth is undebatable.

That is what makes Zophar so testy with Job. He goes beyond Bildad's confrontativeness and becomes impatient. "Job," he says, "you of all people know how the system works. Why do you think that it should work differently?" Zophar's shockingly direct statement comes in 11:6: "Know this: God has even forgotten some of your sin."

God, Zophar claims, could have done more to Job and would have been completely justified. God is the high and majestic One, the One whose mysteries are unfathomable and whose limits are illimitable.

Their measure is longer than the earth
    and wider than the sea. (11:9)

Zophar is mightily mad at his friend Job. He is offended by the other two, because they have been mild to Job, and he is offended by Job, because he has been getting away with murder. If Job's words were to continue unabated, Zophar thinks, the world would simply be turned topsy-turvy. There would only be chaos. All rules would go down the tubes, and the only truth left would be whatever Job felt was true.

This has to be stopped. Zophar is the true intellectual among the friends, the one who believes that there are consequences to your thoughts and that what you think may hurt you deeply. Zophar therefore marshals all his resources to try to dislodge Job from thinking and saying what he has thought and said. It is a stiff medicine, a medicine that tastes awful. But if it is necessary to bring Job to health, then let it be administered. This is Zophar's approach to Job.

A Few Words About Job's Response

It takes at least two people to argue. The friends do not speak in a vacuum. They speak to Job, a man whose experience and beliefs we have studied in this book. *Job* also contributes to the conversation and, in fact, contributes to its breaking down. The conversation ends up being like the journeys of two ships passing in the night, almost oblivious to the presence of the other. The friends contribute to the conversation's breakdown through their judgmental attitudes; Job contributes to its breakdown by his insulting words.

Job insults his friends' intelligence, their expressions of concern and their arguments to defend God. Perhaps his greatest insult is that he ultimately ignores them. At the end it is only Job who speaks. The three friends finish their speeches in chapter 25 (with a six-verse speech of Bildad). Job speaks then for six uninterrupted chapters—the longest continuous domination of the "floor" for the whole book. By this time the friends have become unimportant for Job's case; what he must do is find God and speak with him.

Note how Job insults his friends' intelligence. After they had each had a chance to speak, Job mocks them:

Doubtless you are the people,
   and wisdom will die with you!
But I have a mind as well as you;
   I am not inferior to you.
Who does not know all these things? (12:2-3)

Job is contemptuous of his friends, especially their claim to wisdom:

What you know, I also know;
   I am not inferior to you. (13:2)

His attack on their intelligence, however, comes only after he feels that they have betrayed him. More than anything, this feeling causes the conversation to rupture. The friends think they are trying to be *helpful*. Job feels that they are *harmful*. Listen to his words in 6:14-15:

A despairing man should have the devotion of his friends,
   even though he forsakes the fear of the Almighty.
But my brothers are as undependable as intermittent streams.

In a fit of pique and bitterness, Job blurts out,

You would even cast lots for the fatherless
   and barter away your friend. (6:27)

Job is accusing his friends of selling a friend for money, of taking possession of a child whose guardians are unable to pay debts. In short, Job says that his friends love money much more than they love him. They willingly and eagerly sacrifice him. One can hear the barely suppressed accusation of Job: how much are you guys making for abandoning me?

Finally, however, Job insults them by speaking to God alone. He feels that his friends do not and perhaps cannot understand him. His pain has taken him to a different level of life, a level that doesn't seek answers even though it seeks to talk. Job's trouble is so deep that he simply cannot hear the words of his friends. His pain makes him insensible to almost everything else. Isn't that sometimes our situation? We become so preoccupied with our situation that we cannot hear another. So the friends and Job retreat into their private spaces and worlds, after an intense conversation that really has met no one's needs. The entire conversation calls out for yet another party to resolve it—God.

Lessons from the Conversation About Friendship
An old African proverb says, "Friends are so valuable that you should hold onto them with both hands." We might be tempted, by reading the story of Job, to think the opposite. Friends, here, contribute to each other's misery and not to their blessing. Yet there are some enduring lessons about friendship that the book of Job teaches us today.

Friendship is a process and a journey. Friends stay with each other during the journey, no matter how rocky the way or intense the heat. Someone has said that after the age of forty there is not much worth living for except friends. Adversity is not simply the test of friendship; it often is the only way that true friendship is revealed. Friendship has its phases, its joys as well as its painful moments. I think it is significant that even though Job and his friends had the strongest of disagreements, they were all around at the end of the book! No one got up to leave. Even when all fell silent because the young man Elihu wanted to speak (Job 32—37), they all remained. Friends are for keeps; don't leave without them.

All friends come to the conversation with their own private issues. No one is pure. No one sees life objectively. No one can simply give "the truth" and expect the others to meekly acquiesce in that judgment. We tend to think that everyone in the book of Job should subordinate his own needs and desires to those of Job, since Job was so severely afflicted. But people simply cannot do that. We bring ourselves to whatever conversation we have. We bring our joys and triumphs, but also our fears and inadequacies. We bring with us the many ways we try to make order in our chaotic world. When Zophar is so offended at Job in chapter 11, it is partially because Job's complaint disturbs the neat order of the world that Zophar would like to see.

Friendship is incomplete without God. That is a message we need to hear today. We base our friendships on so many other things than God: on likes and dislikes, similar situations in life, common commitments for personal or public good, but we often do not measure our friendships by how they enhance or increase our understanding of God. Job and the friends came to an impasse because everybody *thought* he understood what God was doing, but no one actually invoked God's presence. Job defiantly laid his case before God; the friends had all the wisdom they needed from the traditions of the past.

What our world needs today is people who are not ashamed to say that the basis of friendship is in God. God, in the book of Job, is a living and powerful presence, the One who speaks with authority and intimacy, who desires the restoration of his creatures even as they sometimes live in torment and uncertainty. Bring God into your friendships, for that completes the divine triangle of you, the friend and God. It offers the possibility of deepening the relationships and our understanding, as well as our growth in the knowledge of God. We have a heart-shaped vacuum in our lives for friends and for God; open your heart again today for both to enter.

Prayer
Our loving God, friendship is such a joyful and troubling thing for me. I think of friends you have given, and I am overwhelmed with gratitude for the strength they have provided. I could not have gotten through tough times of life without them. But friendship also troubles me. I know that someday my friendships will end, and that many of them will end not because I choose, but because nature intervenes. Why do you give us each other, only to take each other away, O God? Please help me to

receive people into my life as potential friends, as gifts from you to help me on life's way. May I seek your friendship in all my human ties. And grant, my God, that I would exult in the friendship of Jesus Christ, who called us his friends, and who died so that I might live. It is in his name that I pray, amen.

Questions for Study and Discussion

1. Tell the stories of one or two friendships you have developed over the years.

2. How have you lost some friendships?

3. How have friendships enriched your life?

4. Are you a person who feels more comfortable with hundreds of acquaintances or with a few strong friends? Why?

5. Do you think that our approach to Job and his friends—not assessing blame, but looking at the conversations as an example of how friendship operates—is helpful?

6. How can you make God a more real part of your friendships?

PART 3

RESTORING
HOPE

JOB 33:1-2
But now, Job, listen to my words;
    pay attention to everything I say.
I am about to open my mouth;
    my words are on the tip of my tongue.

7

DREAMING
THE IMPOSSIBLE
DREAM

Seven years ago Deb and her husband Robert received news that Robert had been diagnosed with brain cancer. It was a particularly virulent cancer, and the doctors sadly told them that Robert had only two to four weeks to live. It did not give them much time to face the tragedy. Deb had a personal faith, but it was not particularly vital for her life. Yet when she faced the mountain of Robert's illness, she had to approach God with her need. She felt somewhat awkward doing so— "God, I don't really have the right to come to you, since I haven't been so faithful to date"—but she prayed for healing and wisdom and God's presence. Heavy on her mind was the future of raising two sons, seven and eight at the time, on her own.

Days turned into weeks, and Robert did not die. But he became no better. Deb's prayers, as she realizes now, were prayers for her own needs: "Don't take him, God. He's mine!" Finally, their prayers for healing gradually gave way to prayers for acceptance as Robert's condition worsened. Ten months after the original diagnosis, Robert died.

The process of letting Robert go was difficult. Deb describes how she actually had to let go twice, once when he died and once about a year later. On the anniversary of Robert's death she decided the best way to try to get beyond her loss was to take the boys on a vacation; perhaps, she felt, this would help them all get on with their lives. It didn't work. Memories and grief came back to occupy her mind and heart. She prayed for patience, but she wanted patience right now. And it did not come easily.

Yet she knew, as month succeeded month, that God was there. He provided comfort and friends. Gradually her faith became stronger, and she began to feel that God not only was watching over her but was actively involved in shaping her life and the life of her boys for good. She moved to Wichita and got a job in fundraising in the health-care field. Deb is by nature an outgoing person, and the challenge of a respected job in a vital field, coupled with her newly restored faith, made her feel that life was on the mend. She could begin again.

She met Barry shortly thereafter, and they were married in a Christmas wedding. Life was beginning to take a positive turn. She was stronger for her trials. She trusted God for the future. It seemed as if healing had taken place.

Then came 1993. Deb, Barry and the boys, now in their early teens, had moved to a smaller town, and both Deb and Barry found new jobs. Deb soon began to notice that her grip was not as firm as it should have been and that she forgot details on the job that she normally remembered easily. One morning she became almost terrified because she couldn't use the phone and fax machine. Her limbs grew numb. She went to the doctor and discovered the alarming truth that her silicone breast implants, which she had received after a mastectomy in 1976, had ruptured. Her body was reacting to the effects of silicone poisoning.

Deb smiles ironically when she says that implants, put in to make her feel and look more attractive in 1976, were now possibly endangering her life. She began to worry that her younger son, born after the mastectomy, might suffer some of the side effects of being a "silicone child." She began to wonder about God and why he seemed to be paying so much attention to her in the pain category. Had she been doing something wrong? She solemnly wished that she didn't have to travel this road with death a second time, but she wondered if she was now feeling what Robert had felt four years earlier. She and Barry wept and held each other, and Deb remembers how reassuring his vocal prayers were in the long nights of loneliness and worry. Deb calls her tears her "rainbow to heaven," because they reach directly to the throne of God. At first she worried how Barry would react, since he didn't know fully what he was getting into when they got married. Barry, however, has been a tower of strength for her and the boys.

They knew she would face immediate and very dangerous surgery in Houston, but for several weeks they could not get the operation scheduled. There was a distinct possibility that Deb would die *waiting* for surgery. She was told that her chances for "complete or near complete" recovery were less than 1 percent. Finally late in 1993 she had a ten-hour surgery in which they tried to remove the silicone and reconstruct some of her breasts with stomach tissue.

Deb returned to Kansas and has, with Barry, the boys and her church and community, begun the long process of recovery. She attends meetings of women similarly afflicted and shares her hope in God as well as her sense that her life has taken on a fully different meaning since her surgery. God is more real to her than ever before. Each day is a gift of grace, an opportunity for ministry, a means for God to show his love through her.

One other unexpected dimension has also developed. Deb has never been a "political" person, but she is finding that the combination of her hopefulness, honesty, faith and frankness is drawing her into the arena of public policy. She is angry, she confesses, at the companies who knowingly continued to manufacture a dangerous substance; she is desirous of supporting the women and families of those similarly affected; she feels God is leading her to fight the culture that says to young women that they ought to have this surgery for cosmetic purposes. Deb is a woman who now lives a focused and faithful life, a life of hope when it would have been so easy to have abandoned hope. She dreams impossible dreams because she has been brought through some deep valleys and has emerged on the other side. She and Barry truly believe that God is there with her in the valleys and that God is very active in her daily life. Hope is real in the midst of life-threatening problems.

Job's Hope

I would like us to keep Deb's story in mind as we reflect on our hope and Job's hope. Throughout Job's time of distress and anger, of grief and depression, of audacity and frustration, there are moments of hope which rise from the text like a great mountain rising from the plain, like Mount Hood or Mount Rainier above the Cascade Range, like Chimney Rock above the Nebraska plains, like Devil's Tower above the Wyoming rangeland. At first the expressions of hope are mere glints; later they turn to glimmers and glances and finally fully fleshed-out visions of hope. By the time he gets to the final expression of hope, his final impossible dream in Job 19, his affirmation that his Redeemer lives, Job is confident and even overwhelmed by the strange and wonderful future that awaits him. His wildest dreams become the sober reality of the New Testament and the bedrock affirmation of Christian faith. Job's wild dream becomes our solid hope. Job's wished-for Redeemer is our Christ, the one who died and lives so that we might live with him.

Hope is a necessary ingredient in human life. The King James Version translation of Proverbs 29:18 captures it best: "Where there is no vision, the people perish."

Without the ability to hope and dream, we humans are lost. Hope is what drives us on; it urges us to try once more, to smile again, to reach out to help, to continue to believe in people. Hope gives shape to our longings and direction to our everyday existence. When we hope, we believe that there still is a future, and that we will have a role to play in it.

A Special Speech

One of the most dramatic and hopeful examples of American oratory is

144

Martin Luther King Jr.'s "I Have a Dream" speech. Spoken in the shadow of the Lincoln Memorial in Washington, D.C., on a sweltering August afternoon in 1963, the speech is a testament to the strength of dreams and hope in the midst of the sobering realities of oppression and racism. What makes the speech particularly effective is the linking of Christian hope and American values.

Many of us can still hear the rich cadences of Dr. King's voice as we listen to phrases from that speech. The reality of Dr. King and many of his listeners was one of near hopelessness. He says,

> I am not unmindful that some of you have come here out of great trials and tribulations. Some of you have come fresh from narrow cells. Some of you have come from areas where your quest for freedom left you battered by the storms of persecution and staggered by the winds of police brutality.

So he urges his listeners to go back to the same places where they were hurt and to believe that somehow their situation will be changed. "Let us not wallow in the valley of despair."

Then comes the great transition paragraph of his speech, the paragraph that catapults speaker, listener and reader into a new plane, as when an airplane breaks through a mantle of clouds on its ascent and is bathed in the blinding and glittering light of the sun. Our hearts start to sing and our yearnings are intensified when we hear,

> I say to you today, my friends, that in spite of the difficulties and frustrations of the moment, I still have a dream. It is a dream deeply rooted in the American dream.

It's a dream, a hope, a vision that he could not see physically but could imagine with the mind's eye and the heart's throb. It is a dream that

> one day on the red hills of Georgia the sons of former slaves and the sons of former slaveowners will be able to sit down together at a table of brotherhood . . . that my four children will one day live in a nation where they will not be judged by the color of their skin but by the content of their character.

King's final dream statement links his hope for America's future with the prophetic word from Isaiah 40.

I have a dream that one day every valley shall be exalted, every hill and mountain shall be made low, the rough places will be made plain, and the crooked places will be made straight, and the glory of the Lord shall be revealed, and all flesh shall see it together.

We can almost imagine the joyful strains of Handel's *Messiah* in the background as we share King's dream in the foreground of the speech. His dream is his hope.

This is our hope. . . . With this faith we will be able to hew out of the mountain of despair a stone of hope.

After rooting his dream in the American dream and his hope in the biblical hope, King finishes by longing for the freedom that is found in both American and biblical affirmations. "Let freedom ring" becomes the phrase that guides him to his peroration in the words of the old Negro spiritual, "Free at last! Free at last! Thank God Almighty, we are free at last!"

Hope and dreams fill the speech. It resonates so deeply in the American and the Christian mind today because of its indomitable hope, its dignified faith, its clear dream and its haunting phrases. Some would say that the ability to hope when things look hopeless is a sign of unrealistic thinking, but King and all those who believe in a better future would say that the essence of biblical hope is to yearn for and visualize that which cannot now be seen. We are all in King's debt precisely because he did not give up hope even in the "sweltering summer of the Negro's legitimate discontent." He dreamed the impossible dream, a dream which is still far from being realized, but one which will fuel every subsequent generation of civil rights workers and every heart of those who want to overcome America's racially torn past.

A Hopeful Poem

For those who would like to hope and continue to dream, even amid temptations to give up or lose hope, Emily Dickinson has a memorable poem. I remember that the first time I shared this poem with an adult education class, one of the women in the class saved it and taped it to her computer, at which she worked daily, as a reminder of the power of hope. I supplemented it there, as I will here, with explicit Christian expressions of hope; yet it speaks in a special, powerful and light language that we need today. Listen to her poem:

Hope is the thing with feathers—
That perches in the soul—
And sings the tune without the words—
And never stops—at all—
And sweetest—in the Gale—is heard—
And sore must be the storm—
That could abash the little Bird
That keeps so many warm—
I've heard it in the chillest land—
And on the strangest Sea—
Yet, never, in Extremity,
It asked a crumb—of Me. (poem 254)

Hope is likened to an indwelling bird that hums a wordless tune, that keeps singing amid the storms of life, and that accompanies us through our chill and strange journeys. But even more, hope is portrayed as something that is always giving and never demanding. Wherever we go, whatever the pressures of life, hope is there to encourage and lift us.

A few years ago my family got a dog, a beautiful golden retriever puppy. We had heard that a retriever would be good with children, so we decided to get one. It was the first dog we ever had. I had grown up with cats and, I have to confess, had never found their finicky, lazy and somewhat demanding ways endearing. As a matter of fact, my experience with cats influenced my perspective on the acquisition of a dog. The family vote was three to one in favor of a dog. I voted in opposition.

Of course we got the dog. At first I decided that I was not going to go out of my way to make friends with it. After all, I figured that the three who voted in favor of the dog should spend their every waking moment with it. But as days turned to weeks and months, I noticed two distinct

developments regarding Murphy, our retriever. First, the three who voted for the dog were not as eager to do all the things necessary to make
life for us and Murphy comfortable. And second, I began, somewhat
against my will, to like the dog. I noted that she was always ready to greet
me when I returned from work, when I awoke in the morning, when I
came home at any time. Actually, she seemed *excited* that I was back. She
was unfailingly ready to take a walk, to come to me to be stroked, or to
listen to me when I wanted to say something that I knew she couldn't
understand but that I wanted to say nevertheless.

Murphy became, in some ways, my "thing with feathers," the thing
that didn't perch in my soul but that always perches in front of me. She
asks nothing of me, except for food, and whenever I want to give anything to her, she receives it with gratitude that exceeds most demonstra-
tions of human thankfulness. When I think of Emily Dickinson's poem
now, I think of my faithful and *hopeful* dog Murphy.

Our Christian Hope

Before looking at how Job's hope emerged in the midst of his despair, I
would like to show with three brief examples how hope and dreams are
an essential thread of our biblical faith.

Consider Abraham and Sarah, the parents of the faithful. They went
out from a city, far from the Promised Land, with no clear sense of where
they were going, to another city, whose builder and maker was God
(Hebrews 11:8-10). Abraham offered his only son on the altar to God,
believing that "God could raise the dead, and figuratively speaking, he did
receive Isaac back from death" (Hebrews 11:19). Paul, in commenting on
his life, says of Abraham,

> Against all hope, Abraham in hope believed and so became the father
> of many nations. . . . Yet he did not waver through unbelief regarding
> the promise of God, but was strengthened in his faith and gave glory
> to God. (Romans 4:18-20)

Our faith is rooted in those who hoped and dreamed, in those who set
out for unseen areas and did strange things in the name of the hope and

148

the dreams and the God who called them.

Then there is Jesus, the Christ. Chosen by God for a huge task, rejected by people whom *he* had chosen, as well as by the religious and secular leaders of the day, turned over to a painful death by a person he loved, Jesus still hoped. He foretold his resurrection, the spreading of the good news of the gospel, the hope that many would find through his name. Bearing the brunt of this rejection and forsakenness (remember his words on the cross, "My God, my God, why have you forsaken me?"— Mark 15:34), Jesus still knew he would be vindicated and satisfied and that God would be glorified in his death. Jesus was a person of great hope, even in the darkest days of his earthly life.

Finally, we learn lessons about hope in the apostle Paul. When he speaks of the coming resurrection and the freedom to be enjoyed not only by the children of God but by all creation, he says,

> We know that the whole creation has been groaning as in the pains of childbirth right up to the present time. Not only so, but we ourselves, who have the firstfruits of the Spirit, groan inwardly as we wait eagerly for our adoption as sons, the redemption of our bodies. For in this hope we were saved. But hope that is seen is no hope at all. Who hopes for what he already has? But if we hope for what we do not yet have, we wait for it patiently. (Romans 8:22-25)

In two verses Paul uses the word *hope* five times. The hope of ultimate redemption is the anchor which gives us confidence today to work and play and dream in God's service. The Christian hope "perches in the soul," and speaks quietly yet firmly to us throughout our life. Though we have been beat up or cut up by the rough places of life, though our eyesight dims and our limbs grow weaker and our energy wanes, we have a sure, steady and life-giving confidence that through Christ our best days are to come—if not here, then with him in glory. We are free to labor and pray, to dream and hope, to struggle and care, because our eternal destiny is secure. Someone has said that those most ready to die are those most ready to live. So we are delivered over to life *here and now*, with all its promise and pain, because we are assured of life *there and then*. Thanks be to God!

Job's Struggling Hope

From what we know of Job and his situation, we are a bit surprised that he can even hope. He has repeatedly stated his hopelessness and desire to die. Though we have also witnessed his feistiness and boldness, we said that Job seems to be bold because he has nothing to lose, because he *cannot* be reduced to anything less than he already is. Yet, in this section we meet Job again and see a man who struggles with hope and who through struggle wins! It is as if two monstrous creatures, hope and despair, are locked in mortal combat—and hope, the unlikely one, finally wins. Job's struggle to maintain his hope in the unlikeliest of situations, gives us strength, direction and confidence to hold fast to our firm anchor of hope, our Lord Jesus Christ, in our struggles.

To show how difficult and ambiguous Job's hope is at first, I will quote a verse that seems to teach *contradictory* things about hope. The New International Version, which we have been using in this book, follows the King James and many others in translating a crucial verse on hope, 13:15, as follows:

Though he slay me, yet will I hope in him;

I will surely defend my ways to his face.

Job seems to be saying, at least in this translation, that he will hope in God no matter what comes along. Let goods and kindred go, this mortal life also. No matter what, I will continue to hope in God, even as I make my case to him.

Yet the Revised Standard Version and an increasing number of the best biblical scholars translate the verse as follows:

Behold, he will slay me; I have no hope;

yet I will defend my ways to his face.

The strength of this translation is that it makes Job appear consistent. He believes elsewhere that God is out to get him; he expresses his belief elsewhere that he has no hope. This translation stresses the point I have

been making throughout this book—that Job approaches God with boldness because he feels he has nothing to lose.

I really cannot solve this hotly debated translation issue here. No one
can. What I can do, however, is to suggest that a way to understand the
scholarly debate is to see it as an indication also of *Job's* indecisiveness
regarding his future hope. Scholars are confused because *so is Job!* Hope
wrestles passionately with nonhope, and for quite a while it is not clear
which is going to prevail.

Isn't that frequently the way it is with us? Don't both hope and hopelessness clamor for attention and demand the last word in our lives? Isn't
it a struggle sometimes to maintain hope?

I was talking recently with a friend, a single mother of three who
teaches special education at a local elementary school. She was on
summer break and did not really have to begin her daily activities until
about 9:00 a.m. One morning she decided to stay in bed until 8:00 instead
of the usual 6:30. She found, much to her distress, that the longer she
stayed in bed the more depressed she became. At first she wanted to
"sleep in," to recuperate and *gain* strength. She discovered, in contrast,
that staying in bed actually made her think about all the things in her life
that she couldn't control. Thus her great plans for peace ended with
frustration and restlessness. She *had* to get up right away!

Hope and hopelessness are like two vain siblings that both demand
priority and immediate attention in our lives. Job's situation is our situation, only expressed in a more eloquent form.

We will study four brief passages in Job to understand both his struggle
to maintain hope and the "impossible" dream that he sees in his mind's
eye.

There Is No Umpire! (Job 9:33-34)

In chapter 9 Job has been entertaining the idea of approaching God with
his complaint. He knows he has a valid point, but he is also quite sure
that God would not be sympathetic to him and would reject his claim out
of hand. Job says, "Even if I summoned him and he responded, I do not

believe he would give me a hearing" (v. 16). Yet Job knows instinctively that something is wrong. *God, he thinks, really is not an unjust and cruel God. He really would listen to reason!* Still, the power of hopelessness is winning in his life at this stage. Job longs for someone, somewhere, to help out, and he expresses this hope for a brief moment:

If only there were someone to arbitrate between us,
to lay his hand upon us both,
someone to remove God's rod from me,
so that his terror would frighten me no more. (vv. 33-34)

But Job expresses his desire in what grammarians call a "contrary to fact wish." What that means is that even though Job is expressing a desire for something (someone to arbitrate), he *knows* that there is no such person. It is like someone saying, "If only it would stop raining," right in the middle of a downpour that will not let up for hours. Job has some hope here, or he wouldn't even have thought about a possible arbitrator, but the hope is quickly extinguished, as quickly as a whispered word disappears into a howling gale.

At this point in the book Job feels the hopelessness that washes over us before we have had a chance to rebuild or even think about rebuilding. It is the feeling that many Midwestern people felt in the summer of 1993 as the Mississippi River and its tributaries washed away their homes and farms: "If only I could wake up and discover that this big flood was nothing more than a dream!" But it was not a dream; nor is Job's disaster a dream.

Resignation and Hope (Job 14)

Job's quest for hope reaches its most eloquent expression in Job 14. In this passage Job reflects on and laments the fleeting and fixed nature of human life. We are like hired hands who work our time and then are gone. We do not rise again, and we sleep an eternal sleep (vv. 1-12).

The tree, in contrast, has hope for future life; if it is cut down, it will live again. But we will not. At this point in the poem, we recognize that Job has returned to the thought of Job 9. *Things ought to be different*, he thinks. Just as there *ought* to be an arbitrator, though there isn't, so there *ought* to be a future life for us. Job squashed the idea in chapter 9 before he had an opportunity to develop it, but what is remarkable about Job 14 is that Job entertains his hope a bit longer. Job will let his mind play out his hope for a future life and will let his imagination run wild with a scenario of how such a life might be lived. He imagines a pleasant time of renewal, when God will call and he will answer, when God will cover his sin because of restored intimacy. He can almost *taste* it. Listen to Job's words:

> If a man dies, will he live again?
>> All the days of my hard service
>> I will wait for my renewal to come.
> You will call and I will answer you;
>> you will long for the creature your hands have made.
> Surely then you will count my steps
>> but not keep track of my sin.
> My offenses will be sealed up in a bag;
>> you will cover over my sin. (14:14-17)

Job wants such a restored intimacy *so much!* Instead of Job calling God to the witness stand in a judicial proceeding, as Job is planning, God would call *him* to discipleship and renewed trust. Just as God called Moses at the burning bush, or just as he called the people out of the land of Egypt into the Promised Land, so God would call on Job! And Job, like the eager boy Samuel in the service of Eli, would answer with joy and purpose. *Oh*, Job thinks, *wouldn't it be wonderful if we could move from a judicial to a covenantal setting, just God and me!*

But Job's hope is not yet strong enough that it triumphs over his hopelessness. He continues with language of great strength and emotion, but also language of great and hopeless finality.

> But as a mountain erodes and crumbles
>> and as a rock is moved from its place,
> as water wears away stones
>> and torrents wash away the soil,

so you destroy man's hope. (14:18-19)

Such grim pessimism! Such a mournful conclusion! Yet I believe that Job is not quite as hopelessly lost as he appears. Sometimes our most desperate verbal expressions of hopelessness do not match our actual condition. I know that one of the bleakest conversations that my wife and I had about our marriage and relationship was just before we arrived at a very positive and more lasting resolution to some of our difficulties. The same is true for Job here. He appears to be exhausted and utterly without hope. But he is thinking about what it would be like to have things differently. A breakthrough is not far away.

The Breakthrough (Job 16)

The night is darkest before the dawn, and Job's complaint never gets bleaker than in chapter 16. We have already studied the vicious attack language of 16:7-14, where Job says that God has pierced, shattered and torn him. Then Job relates his own weeping and mourning and sense of personal purity. He feels that he did nothing deserving such harsh condemnation.

The gloves are off. He has nothing to lose. He calls on the earth, the everlasting and firm foundation beneath, to confirm the truth of his words.

> O earth, do not cover my blood;
>> may my cry never be laid to rest!
> Even now my witness is in heaven;
>> my advocate is on high.
> My intercessor is my friend
>> as my eyes pour out tears to God;
> on behalf of a man he pleads with God
>> as a man pleads for his friend. (vv. 18-21)

These words constitute a breakthrough for Job because now his *wish language* changes to *certainty language*. My witness *is* in heaven. No longer does he have to express hopes that are dashed or wishes that must be unfilled or thoughts that have no future to them. Now he expresses his words in the present indicative. It is the language of fact.

We need to examine the nature of this fact Job is proclaiming, for this fact revolutionized not just Job's life, but the nature of faith itself. Job affirms that he has a heavenly witness who will argue for him and support him in that sphere. This heavenly witness is a friend who will plead for him before God. The remarkable truth is that Job envisions a *second* figure in heaven, who will be his advocate in his case before God. His breakthrough is his belief that there must be a friendly figure up there. His understanding of God and of faith and of the universe *requires* a heavenly friend and advocate. In the wrestling match between despair and hope, hope now has the upper hand. Hope has, as it were, reversed his negative position. In competitive wrestling, you get one point for an escape and two points for a reversal. Chalk up two points for Job.

So vivid, compelling and powerful is this picture of an advocate in heaven for us that the New Testament picks up on it and refers to Christ as our advocate. Listen to the language of 1 John: "My dear children, I write this to you so that you will not sin. But if anybody does sin, we have one who speaks to the Father in our defense—Jesus Christ, the Righteous One" (2:1).

In Hebrews 7:24-25 Jesus is also called the one who intercedes for us. "But because Jesus lives forever, he has a permanent priesthood. Therefore he is able to save completely those who come to God through him, because he always lives to intercede for them."

Job's courage to hope in the face of the most brutal injury places us all in his debt. His hope for a heavenly defender and intercessor, born out of the pain of his distress, is now our most cherished belief. Pain has driven him to clarity and wisdom.

I Know That My Redeemer Lives (Job 19)

But this is not the end of Job's story of hope. He visits the topic once more. In chapter 19 Job reiterates God's attack on him and then laments how his friends have deserted him and his kin have gone away (vv. 1-20). He is "nothing but skin and bones." He has escaped with only the skin of his teeth (v. 20). In this horrendous condition, he does two things: he asks his friends for pity, and he expresses the wish that his words would be preserved forever (vv. 21-24).

Then comes the dramatic affirmation:

I know that my Redeemer lives,
    and that in the end he will stand upon the earth.
And after my skin has been destroyed,
    yet in my flesh I will see God;
I myself will see him
    with my own eyes—I, and not another.
How my heart yearns within me! (vv. 25-27)

My words here cannot hope to catch the combination of certainty, hope, vision, overwhelming grace, dreaming and longing that characterize these verses. The Hebrew text is almost impossible to translate. I think that is because Job's heart is palpitating so wildly here that it is like trying to speak clearly when you are completely out of breath. He is overcome by the vision. My Redeemer (the same as "my witness" in 16:19) lives. The heavenly figure is not simply an advocate but a deliverer, a savior, a redeemer from whatever bondage in which you find yourself.

Not only is he a heavenly figure, but one day he will stand on the earth. Then Job is carried to the heights of inspiration and imagination and dreaming, and he sees a time that he will see God after his own death, perhaps through the work of the Redeemer. Job will see God or the Redeemer, the text is not clear. Maybe the reason the text isn't clear is that the Redeemer and God are beginning to run together in Job's consciousness. Maybe the two are really one! Maybe Job will get to see all this someday, in a new body! No one in ancient Israel has thought these thoughts before Job, much less whispered them or written them. But Job does.

And then it is too much for him. Like a great teacher who has given all she has in a lecture, or a great athlete who has expended himself completely in a contest, so Job, our spiritual warrior, our hero of the spirit, is fully overcome. Another translation of the last phrase is "My inmost being is consumed with longing!" (Clines, *Job 1—20*, p. 428) or "My heart faints within me!" (RSV). He is utterly spent, totally exhausted, fully consumed.

Yet the exhaustion is the exhaustion of fulfillment and of vision. Job has seen things that no human being has seen. He has insights that were not given to another. He develops these insights when he hopes, when he refuses to give up to the demands of his own body and the pain of his suffering. He knows that his Redeemer lives because, fundamentally, he knows God almost as well as God knows himself. He has been deeply hurt and he will be deeply healed, and one of the instruments of that healing is his unquenchable hope, a hope that only emerged in the middle of the book of Job, but that after that point gave him vision and power and strength to see things through to their completion. Thanks be to God for the hope and courage of Job!

Learning from Job's Hope

Our method in this book is to see Job as our sage counselor and wise guide and to try to understand how his experience of grief and faith and hope teaches us about faith today. The apostle Paul stresses the same truth when he says, "For everything that was written in the past was written to teach us, so that through endurance and the encouragement of the Scriptures we might have hope" (Romans 15:4).

We need all the help we can get to live faithfully today. Job provides it for us. I think that Job's approach to hope offers us at least three truths today.

There is no future in hopelessness. This may seem like an obvious point, but it needs to be made. If anyone had good reason to feel bitter and hopeless, it would be Job. Every blessing human and divine was his. He had every reason to believe it would continue. But it didn't. He feels and expresses his anger and bitterness in unforgettable terms. He also walks through the valley of hopelessness. Yet he realizes that though hopelessness may have its initial attractiveness (haven't you felt the "rush of power" in expressing your anger or hurt or isolation?), hopelessness really does not have any long-term rewards or satisfactions. Hopelessness cannot ultimately affirm life, because at its root it says that life is not worth living.

We need to hear that message of Job today. *I* need to hear it. The strange allure of hopelessness catches me in its net all too often. I sometimes feel as if I am stuck or trapped, unable to extricate myself from a tangled web of painful relationships and commitments. I sometimes feel sorry for myself and sink into hopelessness. Yet I have discovered that there is no way out of hopelessness except to restore my hope in God! It may take two or three "runs" at it, as it took Job several chapters to move from hopelessness to tentative hope to full hope, but Job teaches me that my true hope is in God alone, and it is *that* which should entice and allure my heart.

One of the key methods of overcoming hopelessness is through the religious imagination. Job is finally able to maintain his hope because he can *imagine* a future where he will see God in the flesh. Job is not so different from us. We cannot claim that Job was simply blessed with a good imagination and that we are not; therefore, we will have to wallow in hopelessness. No. Job had an imagination because he would not let go of *either* God *or* his religious experience. He knew that God was a powerful and merciful God. He could not let go of that. He knew also that he had suffered terribly and to a degree incompatible with belief that the world was ruled by a merciful God. He would let go of neither belief. He *could* not let go of either belief.

So his mind began to work, putting the two together in the same room, so to speak—a merciful and powerful God and a broken life. He let them look at each other, examine each other, glower at each other and finally speak to each other. His God and his pain were the two most vital realities of his life. Job spoke out his pain to his God, and he kept speaking and kept speaking. Finally hope emerged. The union of God and pain brought hope. Remember, however, that the hope emerged only after two or three attempts. It was not easy or automatic. It was sparked by the religious imagination's *unwillingness* to let go either of God or of the pain.

Job's word to us today, then, is that our religious imagination emerges directly from our experience of God and of living. Don't try to think "deep thoughts." Don't try to convince yourself that only the smart people or the naturally imaginative people have the capacity to dream and hope. *You* do. Job teaches us that imagination emerges from our willingness to let *neither* God *nor* our experience of life go. Hope springs eternal in the human heart when we nurture both our faith in God and our experience of living in this world.

The movement from hopelessness to hope brings understanding and clarity. At first glance this might be a surprising point, since I argued above that Job's hopeful vision in 19:25-27 is very difficult to understand. What I mean, though, is that Job's deep acquaintance with grief, pain, hopelessness and hope led him to think much more clearly and express himself with a depth, penetration and insight that are unparalleled. Pain exacts such a cost from us, but it compensates us with understanding and insight. I have found that the most insightful comments into Scripture and life have come from people who have suffered deeply.

The greatest insight I have gained about despair came from a mother whose son had committed suicide; my most memorable lesson about hope came from a person who had been abused as a child; my most precious insight about family came from a young person who had lost his family. God seems to have so arranged the world that *the prizes of wealth, happiness and understanding all go to different people.* Job teaches us that the school of pain is the best teacher for those who want understanding. Make no mistake about it, though. If those who have suffered deeply were given a choice, they certainly would not have chosen to walk the path that they have. Now that they have walked it, they have an insight, sobriety and perception that set them apart, an insight that may indeed become the gift of God to a generation or, as in the case of Job, to all people until the end of the world. This is Job's hope, and it is also our hope today.

Prayer

God of my life, I need you today. I need to confess that I have lived in hopelessness. I have not embraced or welcomed the promises of your presence in the gospel. I have not welcomed strangers or strange pains that have entered my life. I close myself off to people and you for so many reasons. I am busy. I am struggling with the many demands already on me. I am trying to overcome pain from the past and present. Sometimes I nearly faint because I see no end in sight, no respite at all. Please forgive my hopelessness, my unwillingness to see you as active in my life, my lack of desire to hold on to you and my pain. Kindle a spark of imagination in me, O God, and help me to express my hope in you through words, songs and actions for others. May I grasp you alone as my source of life and hope for the future. Through Jesus Christ our Lord, amen.

Questions for Study and Discussion

1. Would you say that people today are mostly hopeful about the future or that they entertain a great deal of hopelessness?

2. When have you felt particularly hopeful in the past? When have you felt particularly hopeless?

3. What have been the means or methods you have used in the past to bring yourself out of hopelessness?

4. What role do God and your Christian faith play in continuing to provide you "strength for today and bright hope for tomorrow"?

5. Have suffering and pain brought insight for you? What insights have they brought?

6. If you could say something to those in apparently hopeless situations today, what would you say, without being trivial or judgmental?

JOB 40:4
I am unworthy—how can I reply to you?
  I put my hand over my mouth.

8

THINKING
DIFFERENTLY
(JOB 26—31)

J ob has been through the fire, and he still lives. He has witnessed and experienced the collective waves of agony that touched every area of his life. He lost family, possessions, health and peace of mind. Those family members and friends that were not lost may still be sympathetic, but most have either turned against him or simply do not understand him. Job has the feeling that he is shouting in a soundproof room with transparent walls. No one hears him, but everyone can see him, and all, he believes, are making fun of him.

He has expressed his anger, grief, bitterness and hopelessness. He has been both listless and animated, determined and resigned, terrified and unafraid. Thoughts of injustice and betrayal have been raging through his mind. Yet the most curious and amazing thing is that in the chapters we will study now (Job 26—31), Job begins the process of regaining trust. His trust will not be restored easily or painlessly, but it will be restored, and he will ultimately die "old and full of years" (42:17), that is, having lived abundantly, full of satisfaction and gratitude for life.

In the remainder of this book we will look at how Job regains his trust in God, how he is able to move from despair and defiance to confident, restored trust. We will see how Job's process of regaining trusting can be a light for us to understand and begin trusting God again ourselves. For we *can* trust God again, and we *can* take specific steps to do so, and we *can* learn to make it a *daily* practice in our lives of Christian discipleship. We start by learning to seek wisdom.

Searching for Wisdom (Job 28)

By the time Job and his friends begin the third round of speeches in Job 20, they have said almost everything that can be said. They seem to have looked at the problem from every angle; they have repeated themselves at length. In the first two chapters of his final speech (26—27) Job criticizes his friends, describes his pain and hopelessness, finds fault with God and stoutly declares his orthodoxy. He has been doing this for more than twenty chapters, and the perceptive reader can be forgiven for wondering if this dilemma will ever be resolved. Then in Job 28 something happens.

Job 28 is a magnificent hymn to wisdom, a finely crafted poem which rivals Job 14 in its beauty. Job 14 is a poem of great *resignation* because of our transient life on earth; Job 28 is a poem of great *searching* for wisdom. Though Job 28 is not written in prayer form, I believe that this is Job's *prayer to God* for wisdom to resolve his problem. This prayer focuses on three things: the ingenuity of humans in searching out and bringing to light valuable things (vv. 1-11), the inaccessibility of wisdom, even to clever humans (vv. 12-22), and the need for God to reveal true wisdom (vv. 23-28).

Job 28 says in beautiful poetic form what James teaches in didactic form when he says, "If any of you lacks wisdom, he should ask God, who gives generously to all without finding fault, and it will be given to him" (James 1:5). Job realizes that if his situation is to be resolved, he *must* have this divine wisdom. But I need to spell this out a bit more. Many times we ask for God's wisdom or insight, but we really don't think we need it or don't believe it will be forthcoming. We pray for God's wisdom to complete a task or a test, but we are pretty sure that we have the strength to pull it off ourselves. We pray halfheartedly, not with obvious disbelief, but at best with lukewarm expectation. We probably would not know it if we *did* receive divine wisdom.

This is *not* the attitude of Job, nor can it be the attitude of anyone today who wants to regain trust. The first step in regaining trust is to ask sincerely for God's wisdom. You say that you have asked for wisdom. How do you know? Have your efforts been sincere or intermittent? Has it been the focal desire of your heart? The biblical book of Proverbs helps us sort out whether our desires for wisdom have been sincere:

My son, if you accept my words
   and store up my commands within you,
turning your ear to wisdom
   and applying your heart to understanding,
and if you call out for insight
   and cry aloud for understanding,
and if you look for it as for silver
   and search for it as for hidden treasure,
then you will understand the fear of the LORD
   and find the knowledge of God. (Proverbs 2:1-5)

To search for wisdom, divine wisdom, means that the search is the deepest need and most profound longing of the human heart. It is the yearning that shouts, "O Lord, I simply am lost without your insight. I am empty without your knowledge. I know that in me dwells no good thing but in you are all things. Grant me, I pray dear Lord, a portion of 'all things,' grant me the wisdom that only you can give, to see things differently and to trust you fully with my life and with the future."

A New Language

Job needs wisdom because he needs a new language to describe his condition and yearning. One of the ways to look at Job in Job 1—27 is that he is caught in the web of a language that does not suit him anymore. It is a language of fervor and power, but one that his friends can't understand, and one that doesn't bring his problems any closer to resolution. He needs a new way of talking about his distress and his hope.

Job has been through the fire, and the fire has changed him. It has burned him. It has scarred him. It has charred his features. It has left deep, searing scars on his soul. He has not emerged unscathed. He needs to speak now in the agony of his soul. God has "made me taste bitterness of soul" (27:2), and the taste will never leave his mouth. He is a different man. He has experienced life at a different level than his friends. He has seen such powerful things that his former vocabulary is simply not sufficient to describe them. He needs a new speech, a new vocabulary, new verbal tools to capture this completely different world he has encountered.

If you truly desire to regain your trust in God, and to live in the strength of that trust, you must learn a new language. It may be as difficult as learning French or German or even Japanese or Sanskrit. It may be that the language you need to learn is the language of care or of love or of forgiveness or of honesty or of integrity or of trust. You must have the instinctive sense that you *cannot* learn this language on your own; you must have the strength, wisdom and insight of God to do this. You must have God's wisdom to put names on feelings that you never knew you could feel, much less describe.

What is the language you especially need to learn? If you have difficulty forgiving yourself and other people, perhaps it is the language of reconciliation and forgiveness. If you have difficulty accepting and giving love, perhaps you need to learn the language of care. If you have a difficult time owning up to your past and the mistakes you have made, perhaps you need to learn the language of integrity. Tell God which language you need to learn. If you don't even know which language that is, ask God for wisdom. You need to be in an "earnest-search" mode; you need to be near desperation. You need to feel that your other options either are exhausted or are not options at all. You need to feel that without divine assistance, you simply cannot do it. Are you there? If so, then pray for wisdom, and pray for the capacity to speak a new language. If not, then you are not ready yet for what follows. Because the next step to trusting God again is to relive your past with the aid of the newly discovered language.

Reliving the Past

To go forward in trust, you must first go backward. You must learn to tell your own story, with your own words, at your own pace and to your own audience. You must learn to *own* your past, to make it truly *your* past, to claim it as a most vital part of you. You must learn to talk about it, to explain it with words that are *your* words, to tell the truth about it, as you are able to discern that truth.

To make your past your own by learning a new language can be an experience fraught with terror. Sheri, our friend who was sexually abused as a child and adolescent, found this out firsthand. For many years Sheri lived with the awareness that something from her past was not right. She suffered physical ailments and mental depression, but could never put her finger on what had taken all the zest out of life. Only when Ashley, her daughter, reached an age where Sheri herself had started to experience sexual abuse did Sheri reach a crisis point and remember the abuse she had suffered. She sought professional help. She was told to keep a journal of her thoughts. She also was told that she would need to relive, or at least, retell her past.

Hear Sheri's words: "Through the counseling and journaling, I began to unleash all the horror of my memories. I began to remember and relive the incidents and to experience the pain of abuse. Four different perpetrators were brought to mind—two of my brothers, my brother-in-law, and my father, a minister. . . . The next weeks were so harrowing for me. Along with the humiliation I felt at not being able to handle things on my own, I felt emotional pain like I'd never felt before. I remembered night after night of being sexually abused by my father and molested by my brothers. Intrusive touches, lack of privacy, hugs and kisses and fondling that were totally inappropriate. I remembered witnessing my father physically and sexually abuse my sister."

Looking into her past was looking into the yawning abyss of hell itself. Fear, anxiety and hopelessness came back. She tried to commit suicide once by taking pills. "I was on a roller coaster that wouldn't stop," she says. But Sheri realized that by reliving the harrowing experiences of abuse, she was able to survive them. By putting new language to her experience, language that she had never used before, Sheri began to take control of her life and feelings. As she says, "I began to learn how to care for myself instead of letting others take care of me." And then she says, "I acknowledged changes in my ways of thinking." She began to make conscious decisions about herself and her future.

She knew that she was still a mother, a wife and even a daughter. But for the first time in her life she discovered that she was Sheri, a person whose own needs, desires and skills were good and desirable. She remained and still remains confused about many things. She knows that her confusion arises because she needs a new language to incorporate her new ideas and feelings. But the key to regaining trust for Sheri has been to relive her past, even though it literally almost killed her to do so.

Reliving Job's Past (Job 29—30)

Job relives *his* past for all to see in Job 29—30. Out of the bitterness of his soul, he speaks with an absorption and intensity that is almost palpable. Listen to his energy and his enormous yearning:

How I long for the months gone by. . . .

Oh, for the days when I was in my prime. (29:2, 4)

His zeal to describe his past almost eats him up. He simply *must* tell his story. But, wait a minute. Hasn't Job been telling his story all along? Haven't we been hearing Job's words about his distress from the beginning of the book? How can I claim here, then, that Job is *now* telling his story?

This is a key issue and question. The difference between what Job does in Job 29—30 and what he has done before this time is that *in these two chapters Job finally connects his pain with his full past*. In the early chapters of Job, he has been struggling with the intensity of his feelings, his desire for justice *now*, the inhospitality of his friends *now*, the need for healing *now*. In his great anguish of body and soul Job has really become a one-dimensional figure—a sufferer *now*. But that really is not Job! Job is much more than the lonely sufferer, much more than the tormented figure who cries out for justice. He has had a rich life, a life of blessing and meaning, a life filled with good things. The problem for Job is that he needs to *integrate* his painful self into his formerly joyful self and *make one self*. He is a torn and divided person now, and he has to become a united person. The only way he can do that is to tell of his past.

He tells the story of his past and connects it with his present, so that, at least in his telling of his own life, *his present becomes part of his life*. In his distress, Job is living as if the loss was the great exception, the thing that doesn't fit, the thing for which there is no explanation or from which there is no salvation. It is his own private holocaust. But healing can only come for Job if he is able to establish some lines of continuity between the person who suffers now and the person who prospered then. He must search for language that affirms his dignity then and now, that says that he is the same person then and now, that his pain is not simply a grotesque appendage that doesn't belong but that it somehow is part of his life. So he relives his life for us and for himself.

Space does not permit me to give a detailed examination of both chapters, but I would like to highlight how Job remembers his past and how he connects it with his present. My major point is that at this juncture in Job's "trust-building" exercise, there is still a strong discontinuity between past and present. But at least he is talking about them in the same speech. By doing this he is creating the possibility that at a future time, the past and the present may not simply be linked literarily, but also be connected *theologically and psychologically*. So he takes a tiny step in restoring trust, a small effort to reconstitute his world.

Job first speaks about the sweetness and prosperity of his former relationship to God (29:1-6). He yearns for those blessed days,

> when my path was drenched with cream
> and the rock poured out for me streams of olive oil. (v. 6)

Life was so much simpler then. God was such a real and blessed presence. Children and family surrounded him. He walked in the light of God.

His pleasant thoughts continue. In 29:7-17 Job remembers the justice he performed and the honor he received. Make no mistake. Job believes that he was a man who loved justice:

I put on righteousness as my clothing;
  justice was my robe and my turban.
I was eyes to the blind
  and feet to the lame.
I was a father to the needy;
  I took up the case of the stranger. (29:14-16)

All of this added up to honor in the community. When Job spoke, people listened. Young men were deferential; chiefs and nobles hushed to hear him. All thought well of him. It was such a wonderful life that he felt he would be glad to die in this glory and honor (29:18-25).

Now, however, everything is different. The one word that captures the anguish of Job in chapter thirty is *mockery*. He who once was honored is now dishonored. He who once was the *model* for all now is the *mockery* for all. The language is stark and desperate:

The churning inside me never stops;
  days of suffering confront me.
I go about blackened, but not by the sun. . . .
  I have become a brother of jackals. (Job 30:27-29)

Job has certainly not "solved" his past or fully integrated his past and his present, but he has taken the first step, and so is learning to trust God again for the future.

As you relive your past, your experience may be like Job's or like Sheri's or like neither. Your deep past may be a joyful past that has since become unraveled; your past may be a painful one that is stabbing you afresh today with every breath you take. One thing is certain, however: you must learn to make your past your own. You must put your own words on your past, telling it in the order that *you* want to tell it and placing the emphasis where *you* want to place it. Your past is your personal treasure, more valuable than the richest hoard of gold. If you are captive to your past, you will never break out of it.

Your past can be a prison or a prism, in my judgment. It can capture you and render you powerless, or it can be an instrument that refracts light and creates a beautiful rainbow. To learn to trust God again requires you to speak about your past—at length.

Reaffirming Integrity (Job 29—30)

So Job searches his past like we search the attic—looking for traces that tell us who we are. He is on a mission of self-discovery, a quest to understand. He seeks to think new thoughts or to integrate the old thoughts into his present condition. But what he fundamentally desires and finds, even if he didn't realize what he was looking for, is *testimony to his personal integrity*. He is looking for evidence that affirms that he indeed was, and is, a *good* person.

We might think that as Job pores over his past (in Job 29), he appears self-centered and even arrogant at times. All he seems able to do is tell all the great things he has done. He searches for evidence of his past importance. He spoke and people listened. He said, "Jump," and they said, "How high?" But beneath all the posturing and braggadocio, what is at work here is Job's desperate need to discover how he is a person of worth and significance. Job doesn't fully believe the evangelical doctrine that "God puts broken lives together." Perhaps God could help him heal, but that is not happening now, when Job feels God is treating him as if he were worthless, his friends are telling him that he has sinned, his wife tells him to curse God and die. *No one* is reminding him that he was valuable *then* and that he is valuable *now* and that perhaps a link between then and now is his value.

Job has to discover his value on his own. He has to discover for himself whether life is worth living, whether he really stands for anything. He faces himself nakedly and says, "Who are you, Job?" and he answers, "I have lived with integrity." His search, then, is to discover or rediscover his own integrity.

The word *integrity* means "the quality or condition of being whole or undivided; completeness or soundness." We use the word *integer* in mathematics to describe a whole number. An integer differs from a fraction in that the integer is whole and the fractions are "fractured"—broken or partial. Job's entire experience in the book of Job is one of fracturing: "My days have passed, my plans are shattered, and so are the desires of my heart" (17:11). Everything is broken, including his heart.

Living in a condition of brokenness, we soon begin to wonder whether it is not simply our present condition but our *inescapable, irreversible* condition. Job has certainly entertained those thoughts. How could he *not* have entertained them, with his friends all around urging him to confess and "make up" to God?

Yet after diligently searching his past, Job discovers a Job he likes, a Job who is a person of integrity. One key to restored trust is not simply to tell your past in your own words, but to rediscover your integrity. You really cannot trust God again for the future with a vigorous trust unless you believe that you *are* and you *have been* a person of integrity. That does not mean that you have made no errors. That does not mean that you have to convince yourself and others that you have had a perfect past. On the contrary. Even if you have had a checkered past, even if you have done things of which you are not proud, you need to say that those bad things, however embarrassing or wrong, were not the full and adequate expression of who you really are or were. That is, you cannot be made well if you can think of yourself only as a sick person.

In this light we are ready to understand Job's claim to integrity in the right spirit. He knows he isn't faultless, but he claims integrity because he cannot get well without believing in his basic honesty and uprightness. In this belief he is uncompromising:

As surely as God lives, who has denied me justice,
    the Almighty, who has made me taste bitterness of soul,
as long as I have life within me,
    the breath of God in my nostrils,
my lips will not speak wickedness,

and my tongue will utter no deceit.
  I will never admit you are in the right;
    till I die, I will not deny my integrity.
  I will maintain my righteousness and never let go of it;
    my conscience will not reproach me as long as I live. (27:2-6)
He is saying to God that his whole life stands open for inspection. It is
the same spirit of the psalmist when he says,
  Search me, O God, and know my heart;
    test me and know my anxious thoughts.
  See if there is any offensive way in me,
    and lead me in the way everlasting. (Psalm 139:23-24)
"See me in my nakedness, O God," Job says. He is not afraid of what God
will find.

Job's Final Words (Job 31)

Several years ago, Richard Foster argued in his book *Money, Sex and Power*
that these three allurements or deadly sins are still among the most
dangerous snares for us today. He wrote his book in the middle of the
1980s, a decade that many commentators have likened to the Gilded Age
of the 1890s or to the Roaring Twenties—periods in American history of
unparalleled greed and rapacity. Foster was reacting to the overemphasis
on these things in the culture at large by trying to help Christians develop
a more healthy perspective on things that most of us need and many of
us want more of: money, sex and power.

As we study Job's last words in Job 31, I am struck by the fact that Job's
appeal to his own integrity keeps coming back to these three areas. I am
not so sure that I could make the claims that Job does about himself in
relation to money, sex and power. Job claims integrity in words that are
combative, uncompromising and clear. His words remind me of the words
attributed to Martin Luther, father of the Protestant Reformation, when
he was asked at the Diet of Worms in 1521 to recant his beliefs. Luther
responded that unless he was convinced by Scripture or plain reason, he
could not recant. It was not right to go against Scripture or conscience.

"Here I stand," he said. "God help me. I can do no other." In such a spirit Job claims integrity in sexual, power and financial matters.

Before we look at an example of each, note the common structure of all of Job's claims in Job 31. He says, "If I have done something wrong then let others get what I would have received," or "let me suffer by the loss of the offending part." Job is, as it were, raising his right hand and taking an oath and saying to God, "All right. Punish me if I am being untrue to my word. I can take it. I have nothing to hide."

Job holds fast to his sexual purity.

> If my heart has been enticed by a woman,
>> or if I have lurked at my neighbor's door,
> then may my wife grind another man's grain,
>> and may other men sleep with her. (vv. 9-10)

At the beginning of the chapter he says,

> I made a covenant with my eyes
>> not to look lustfully at a girl. (v. 1)

Job is coming very close to fulfilling Jesus' nearly impossible directive in the Sermon on the Mount that requires one not even to look lustfully on another person (Matthew 5:28).

Job also claims integrity in financial matters.

> If I have put my trust in gold
>> or said to pure gold, "You are my security,"
> if I have rejoiced over my great wealth,
>> the fortune my hands had gained . . .
> then these also would be sins to be judged,
>> for I would have been unfaithful to God on high. (Job 31:24-28)

Again, Job is claiming a lot. Remember the story of the rich young ruler in the Gospels. After being told by Jesus that in order to become a disciple he had to sell all that he had and give the money to the poor, he went away sad, because he had great wealth. Then Jesus said to his disciples,

> I tell you the truth, it is hard for a rich man to enter the kingdom of heaven. Again I tell you, it is easier for a camel to go through the eye of a needle than for a rich man to enter the kingdom of God. (Matthew

19:23-24)

According to the testimony of his own integrity, Job is one of the few rich people who would enter the kingdom of God. He owned his possessions; they did not own him.

Finally, *Job claims integrity in matters of power* or, in other words, in ethical relations. He maintains that he has not abused his powerful position, a position he has because of God's blessing, and which has brought him respect and honor, as well as great wealth. We should be clear on the nature of this claim. Job is saying that he didn't use his clout to "make things happen" for himself. He didn't "fix" his children's tickets or oppress those who worked for him, though he could have easily gotten away with it. The public and the private Job were not two different people. The respected and judicious man in the public square was like that at home too.

> If I have denied justice to my menservants and maidservants
>> when they had a grievance against me,
> what will I do when God confronts me?
>> What will I answer when called to account?
> Did not he who made me in the womb make them?
>> Did not the same one form us both within our mothers? (31:13-15)

In a particularly felicitous phrase in another location, Job said, "The man who was dying blessed me; I made the widow's heart sing" (29:13).

This is Job's case. By reliving his past he has been able to tell the story of his blessing and misery. By reliving his past, he has discovered that the only leg on which he has to stand is his integrity. So he brings his integrity before God and asks for a judgment. He would proudly wear the indictment of God (31:35-36), just as the apostle Paul proudly bears on his body the marks of Christ.

Job's words are ended. He knows that he has made his case. What he thinks he wants is the judgment and vindication of God, but what he will eventually get is God himself! Job is becoming ready for God precisely because he is taking steps that lead to the healing of his hopelessness. He knows, with a knowledge that goes deeper than anything, that he is a man of integrity. He has rediscovered that about himself. Once he knows that, and declares it to God, he really does not need to say anything else. The ball is in God's court. The Scripture says it tersely, "The words of Job are ended" (31:40).

Rediscovering Passion

Throughout the book of Job, but especially in those sections where hope is rekindled or trust begins to be restored, the most passionate and intense language appears. Job always speaks the words, and they are words of such longing and intensity that the attentive reader almost weeps. These words teach us that an essential element in restored trust is rediscovering passion for living. The move from despair to trust is such a dramatic transformation of the person that the process *requires* shouts of passion and painful intensity. It is as if the heavenly physician, in healing our souls, needs to use pain to drive out pain, just as Jesus, the good physician, caused shouts of the most dramatic agony to come from the Gadarene demoniac when the demons were leaving him (Mark 5:1-20).

Job is a passionate person. He is passionate about his intellectual search. He is passionate about his quest for justice. He is passionate about defending his integrity. And he is a passionate speaker. Look at two examples of his passionate use of language.

First, just before uttering his hope for a Redeemer, when he feels he is hemmed in and not understood, Job longs for his words to be recorded. The Revised Standard Version translation best captures Job's agony:

Oh that my words were written!
Oh that they were inscribed in a book!
Oh that with an iron pen and lead
they were graven in the rock for ever! (19:23-24)

The only other place in literature I know where three consecutive "Oh's" are used to capture the emotional intensity of the moment is in Sophocles' *Oedipus Rex*, when the truth actually dawns on Oedipus that he has, as the oracle had predicted, killed his father and married his mother. Oedipus's only recourse is to blind himself; he has seen too much of life.

Job is longing for recognition and a hearing with that same kind of intensity.

Second, when Job begins to relive his past (Job 29), he expresses a longing to regain that simple, honorable and prosperous time. His longing is not wistful, pronounced with a faraway look in the eye and a faint, wan smile. It is an intense desire to be returned to that time in his life where things fit together, where he was whole, before his fractured existence began. He says,

> How I long for the months gone by,
>> for the days when God watched over me,
> when his lamp shone upon my head
>> and by his light I walked through darkness!
> Oh, for the days when I was in my prime. (Job 29:2-4)

It is the same intensity of a friend of mine, contemplating an imminent divorce, who poured out his soul to me in longing to return to the easy days of his youth. "Oh," he said, "how I long for those long summer nights when I could listen to the Phillies on the radio and the whole world was just so much simpler and neat!" The raw yearning of my friend ravaged my heart. Job's longing should do the same for all of us.

Finally, when all is said and done and Job has made his case, defended his integrity and relived his past, he says,

> Oh, that I had one to hear me!
> (Here is my signature! let the Almighty answer me!)
> Oh, that I had the indictment written by my adversary! (31:35 RSV)

He so much wants to talk to God, to hear the charges, if any, from *his* lips alone, to stand before God and speak "like a man with his friend." He has, in Pascal's words, a "God-shaped vacuum" in his heart, and nothing, nothing at all except God can fill it.

Our Healing Process

South African author Alan Paton once said, "The tragedy is not that things are broken. The tragedy is that they are not mended again." In this chapter we have seen how Job starts to mend. We don't really know if

Job knows he is starting his recovery process, but it is real nevertheless. It is a healing process that will eventually lead to a restored trust and life for Job, and is a process that is helpful for us today who face the same types of issues as Job in learning how to trust God again for our present and future.

Don't expect to rush the process. Healing and learning to trust again is a slow and gradual thing. Sheri has discovered, for example, that it is taking a long time for her and for her family. I have shown that this is also the case with Job. Trusting God again did not come as a result of a dream in the night or a sudden flash of inspiration. It was a most painful process. It has been so painful for Sheri that, at times, she didn't know whether she would live through it. Job asked God many times to let him die. He wanted God to crush him, to send him into oblivion, so that finally the pain would end and the suffering would be no more. Unless you have been driven almost to the point of wanting to die, you may not be ready for the healing that comes through trusting God again.

Job's healing begins with five steps or stages. We will take the same steps as we begin to heal.

The first is asking for divine wisdom. It can be a prayer as simple as, "Lord, you know how deeply I am sunk in pain. I see no way out. I need your wisdom to see and your power to act so that my healing can take place." Some might consider it foolishness to ask wisdom of God, when apparently all the facts of a situation are there to see and analyze. But the Scriptures teach, "The foolishness of God is wiser than man's wisdom, and the weakness of God is stronger than man's strength" (1 Corinthians 1:25).

God knows the way to wisdom and can provide insight and a new approach that we have not ever conceived. In the next chapter we will discover how the key to Job's recovery came in his ability to listen to God in a new way, in a way he had never anticipated. So ask God for wisdom today. You will not be disappointed.

The second stage or step is to learn a new language. This really will be part of the entire trusting process, but it begins after asking for wisdom. We learn a new language because we have to have words to go with the agony we have endured. Those who refuse to learn a new language are at a loss, just as immigrants to a new country are usually severely hampered if they don't learn the language of that country.

What is the new language that you need to learn in your pain? Tedd and Julie say that their experience of losing their son has given them a language of understanding or tolerance. Before they lost Will, they were very goal-directed and focused, with little time for things that took them or others away from good goals. Now they look on people differently. People are acting the way they are for a reason, they say. It is not good or right just to pass judgment. Maybe their way has been rough. We haven't been in their shoes. If we were there, perhaps we would react the same.

Third, healing begins when you relive your past. An entire book could be written on this alone, but I have stressed that the reason to do this is to seek an explanation of how your life is one fabric, woven together tightly and in a beautiful pattern. Your life is *not* strips of fabrics that don't match, hastily taped together and in danger of coming apart at the slightest provocation. In most instances you will need friends, a counselor or at least a diary to tell this story.

Fourth, the goal of reliving your past is to rediscover your integrity. You cannot be healed and you cannot learn to trust again until you feel that you are a person of value, that you have integrity and wholeness, and that the brokenness you now experience is not the entire story of your life. Job maintained not simply that he was innocent of great crimes, but that his former life had integrity in matters of sex, money and power.

Finally, we need to do all of this with the language of passion. Job knew what it was to be listless and without energy ("what strength do I have, that I should still hope?"—6:11), but he felt also that recovery of trust meant that he had to reaffirm his passion. He *knew* he was a person of passion and intensity in the past. At present he felt its loss, and he needed to rediscover it. He would search for language, wisdom, integrity and his past in such a way that he could rediscover where his passion still lay.

Perhaps this would direct him back to God.

Your passion for living and zest for faith may be waning. You may look wistfully on another time as your golden age or your *annus mirabilis*. But you can rediscover the passion today. Job is living proof that it can be done. You just need to search your life, like a secretary searching the files, for that area in which the passion is still there or can be kindled. The route of your healing, the way to trust God again, will come through the area of your passion.

All is certainly not solved by the end of Job 31. As a matter of fact, from the perspective of an outside observer one could argue that nothing really has changed. But change has occurred. Inner healing and trust-building have begun. Job is learning how to think differently. The next chapter will show how the building of trust continues.

Prayer
Our loving God, thank you that you are in the rebuilding business, and that I cannot go to a better source of wisdom or healing than you. I am often so confused and fractured. I am broken, shattered into so many pieces. I sometimes feel that my life is a series of boxes and that I need to jump from one to another to fill the various roles others expect me to play. I need to trust you again, dear Lord, and to find a unifying center of my life in you. I need to recapture my passion in new words and with new wisdom. Guide me as I search my past, as I try to draw strength and lessons from that time, so that I can be a person of wholeness today. Fill my yearnings, dear God, for they are extreme. Through Jesus Christ our Lord, amen.

Questions for Study and Discussion
1. How and when have you sought wisdom from God? How did you phrase your need?

2. Has the experience of distress taught you any different languages? How has it changed you?

3. We have stated that reliving your past is a necessary and painful step

in regaining trust. Where and under what circumstances have you told your story?

4. What have you learned about yourself by telling your story? What kind of person are you? Are you fractured? How does your present relate to your past?

5. Where is the passion in your life? Where has it gone? How do or did you recover it? How does it drive you each day?

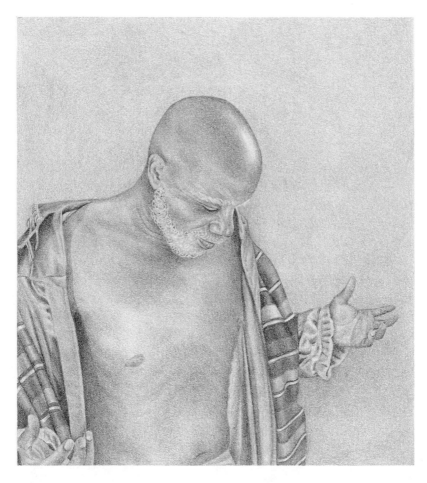

JOB 42:1-2
Then Job replied to the LORD:
"I know that you can do all things;
  no plan of yours can be thwarted."

9

LISTENING & SEEING
DIFFERENTLY
(JOB 32—42)

Trusting God again after great distress means that we need a re-orientation not simply of our thinking but also of our hearing and seeing. We will hear and see things in ways we never conceived, and as we learn to do so, we will sometimes face great disorientation and confusion. We will be tempted to return to simple answers and predictable explanations. But we must realize that God is leading us to find new meaning in our traditional answers, and to explore new avenues of understanding. Trusting God again means that we will need to rediscover our own vulnerability, even as we are trying to defend and strengthen ourselves against new onslaughts of distress.

In Job 32—42, Job moves to a deeper level of knowing God, the level of seeing. At this part of the story Elihu, who has been waiting patiently while his older friends were trying to help Job, takes up the conversation. God, who has been silent since the beginning of the dialogue, also speaks. Through these two persons, one mortal and one immortal, Job learns additional lessons about trusting God again. The breakthrough verse for Job is Job 42:5-6:

My ears had heard of you
  but now my eyes have seen you.
Therefore I despise myself
  and repent in dust and ashes.

We likely will not see God as Job did, but God reveals himself to us in many other ways. Sometimes our new clarity of vision and of hearing comes quite unexpectedly, even unnaturally.

Tedd and Julie's New Eyes

When I visited with Tedd and Julie at their home ten months after the death of their son Will in a farm accident on April 10, 1993, they told me the following story.

Tedd returned to work at the bank on Monday, April 19. In ten days everything had changed for him and Julie and their son, Wes. They had thought they were in control of their lives, but now they knew they were not. They had nothing to replace the empty feeling inside. Tedd, very conservative by nature, is a banker *and* a farmer—a *Kansas* banker and farmer. He did not believe in miracles. He believed in God and hard work and family and tradition, and if you believed in all of these things and worked your tail off, *maybe* the ground would yield for you and your family. That was Tedd's simple but profound creed.

The first day back in the office, Tedd noticed an old man standing outside his office. He was a rancher who did business with the bank but not directly with Tedd. He would see the man about six times a year; they would exchange pleasantries, discuss the price of cattle briefly and then return to their lives. The man was a lifelong rancher, a man in his eighties, a man whose leathery hands and sober demeanor bore witness to his long toil on the Kansas prairie.

Instead of poking his head in Tedd's office to exchange greetings, the man was quietly waiting outside the office. Tedd had a client and could not get to him for about forty-five minutes. Tedd thought, *He is waiting to extend condolences.* Even though they didn't know each other well, the old man would certainly have known that Will had died.

After his client left, Tedd went out to greet the old rancher. The man quietly asked if he could talk to Tedd and Tedd's father, Bill, who was driving the tractor when the accident happened. Bill also worked at the bank. They went into Bill's office and the old man began to talk. He cleared his throat. He was a proud man, a person who knew and taught that you had to be tough to make it in life. He was no sentimentalist. His first words were, "You may think I'm crazy for saying this." Tedd did, at first. Then, he didn't. Here is the old man's story.

"The biggest blessing I have had in life was my wife Margaret. She died last year, and I have been so alone without her. I want to tell you, that though she is gone, Margaret and I still talk to each other."

Tedd distinctly remembers thinking, *Yep, this guy is crazy!*

Then he continued. "While I was talking with Margaret just the other day, she was telling me that they have a new little boy with them. She didn't know his name, but she wanted to tell me about the boy."

A lump began to form in Tedd's throat. Then the man described the boy, and he mentioned five or six distinctive things that only Tedd or Julie would have known about Will. He said, "Margaret told me that she went up to the boy to try to talk to him, but he was very shy and turned away."

Tedd thought, *Sure, that is what Will used to do, but perhaps 50 percent of two-year-olds are shy.*

The old man said, "So Margaret asked him if he wanted something to eat." The old man shook his head. "Margaret said that the boy, though he knew the words, just started to point to everything that he liked and then he ate everything, bread, vegetables, meat, without complaint and very quickly."

Tedd began to think, *This is my boy. This is Will.*

"After the meal," the old man continued, "Margaret tried to put him down for a nap. But he held out both hands, as if to stop her and ward her off." The old man held out his leathery hands straight from his body, as if to imitate the motion of the little boy. Only Tedd and Julie knew that Will did this every time that they tried to put him down for a nap. By this time Tedd was fully absorbed in the story.

"But what I really wanted to tell you," the old man said, "was that later on Margaret was out picking flowers, and the little boy came up to her with his hands behind his back, picked a flower and handed it to Margaret." (Will always walked with his hands behind his back, and he loved to give his mother flowers.) "Then Margaret said to me that the little boy will be fine, and she will take care of him." Without a word, the old man picked up his huge Stetson hat and left. Neither Bill nor Tedd said a word.

Emotionally drained by this time, Tedd dashed out of the office and began walking. *I need some breath,* was all that he could think. *I need to talk to someone. But who?* He headed over to his church, two blocks away. While on the way he thought, *I have* never *spoken to a pastor about anything like this. What will the pastor think of me?*

Tedd entered the church and came into the office of the associate pastor. She was preparing her sermon for the next Sunday and happened to have a book by Frederick Buechner, *The Clown in the Belfry,* on her desk. The book was open to a story of Buechner's dream of a dead friend, a dream in which the friend was very alive and real. After the dream Buechner found a piece of his friend's blue wool sweater in his (Buechner's) bedroom, and there was no way the piece of the sweater could have gotten there by "natural means."

The pastor had been pondering this passage and thinking about the many ways in which her faith had been stretched of late. When Tedd burst in and told his story, it was like a message of God telling *her* to continue looking for traces of the hand of God in out-of-the-ordinary places. Tedd was amazed at her affirmative response, and he rushed home to tell Julie.

Ten months later, when I interviewed them, Tedd and Julie still remember that day vividly. They have taken it to mean two things: that Will is in God's good care and that this universe and God are simply so vast that he sometimes breaks out of our preconceived, limited understanding of him. They see the old man's story as one of the "small miracles" (they now believe in *little* miracles!) that God has brought into their lives since Will's death to confirm his continuing care for them. They have learned to hear and see differently since April 10, 1993.

Tedd and Julie are well aware that some may not believe their story or may even ridicule them for believing it. Before the loss of Will, *they themselves* would have been hesitant to believe such a story. It is important to note that they did not seek this experience or information. The story they heard was completely unsolicited. Its accuracy about Will, its one-time nature, and the fact that it helped rekindle their own Christian faith in a difficult time convinced Tedd and Julie that this story was a gift of God to them. They now believe more strongly than ever that God can and does meet each of us in our moments of need. He has gifts to give all his children. We do not encourage people to seek experiences identical to theirs but rather to be open to the unique, special care that God offers to each of us individually when we struggle with trusting God again after a great loss.

Elihu's Speeches (Job 32—37)

Job, too, learns to see and hear differently. One of the main ways that this happens is through Elihu's speeches. Of course, it will only be after God's two speeches in Job 38—41 that Job experiences a final breakthrough, but Elihu's speeches *prepare* Job to hear God.

At first glance Elihu is the most unlikely person to be a catalyst for Job's restored trust. He, after all, shares the same perspective as Eliphaz, Bildad and Zophar. He is a young man and, therefore, from the perspective of the wisdom tradition, cannot be a possessor of wisdom. He has not said a word to this point, which doesn't augur well for what he may now say.

Yet Elihu brings a freshness and insight that the older men do not possess. One of the ironies of Scripture and of life in general is that the wisdom of God often comes in unexpected places and from unpredictable sources. As the apostle Paul teaches (1 Corinthians 1:27), "God chose the foolish things of the world to shame the wise; God chose the weak things of the world to shame the strong." Elihu is one of the "weak things" God chooses to teach Job and us about trusting him again.

Elihu does three things that none of the other friends do: (1) he *listens* to Job sensitively, (2) he provides a series of possible *explanations* of what Job may be going through, and (3) he suggests an *interpretation* of God's activity in all of this that will lead to Job's freedom. He also states his frank disagreement with Job, but the reader always gets the impression that Elihu is dealing with a person, Job, and not with an abstract idea or a system of doctrine.

Elihu Listens

We can tell that Elihu listened closely to Job because his summary of Job's *complaint* and statement of Job's *condition* is such an accurate restatement of Job's own words. Listen to Elihu's words:

> But you have said in my hearing—
>> I heard the very words—
> "I am pure and without sin;
>> I am clean and free from guilt.
> Yet God has found fault with me;
>> he considers me his enemy.
> He fastens my feet in shackles;
>> he keeps close watch on all my paths." (Job 33:8-11)

Now listen to a few of Job's actual words:

> Do you [God] have eyes of flesh? . . .
>> that you must search out my faults . . .
>> *though you know that I am not guilty.* (10:4-7)
> Why do you [God] hide your face
>> *and consider me your enemy?* (13:24)
> His [God's] anger burns against me;
>> *he counts me among his enemies.* (19:11)
> *You fasten my feet in shackles;*
>> *you keep close watch on all my paths.* (13:27)

I have put the precise verbal similarities between Job's and Elihu's words in italics because it is an indication that *Elihu has been listening.* Job really was not heard by any of his other friends. Job attributes this to his friends' fear of what may happen to them:

Now you too have proved to be of no help;
> you see something dreadful and are afraid. (6:21)

A principal reason for Job's desperation in the earlier chapters is that he feels that *no one* hears him. No one really understands him in his agony. God has absented himself, for some inexplicable reason, and the friends cannot hear him. Job shouts all the louder throughout the book, because he feels he must do so in order for someone, somewhere, to pay attention to him. Finally, someone hears. Elihu shows that he has heard Job's complaint and he understands Job's condition.

Just to make sure that this is not a fluke, Elihu summarizes Job's points a second time:

Job says, "I am innocent,
> but God denies me justice.

Although I am right,
> I am considered a liar;

although I am guiltless,
> his arrow inflicts an incurable wound." (34:5-6)

Who can forget Job's description of God's action against him?

The arrows of the Almighty are in me,
> my spirit drinks in their poison;

God's terrors are marshaled against me. (6:4)

Elihu's summary again is, to use a bad pun, right on target.

Elihu Offers Possible Explanations

Elihu goes further. Perhaps because he has genuinely heard Job, he can go on and offer possible explanations of what is happening. To be sure, the other friends had offered an explanation, but it was one based on the doctrine of retribution. If you suffer, you have sinned. Therefore, confess and be restored. Q.E.D. Ball is in *your* court, Job. This is how the other friends argued.

But Elihu offers three possible explanations of how what has happened to Job is really an example of *God's speaking to Job*. By doing this Elihu takes the issue out of the sin-retribution cycle, which the other friends argue for, and places it into a *conversational* context. The explanations appear in Job 33:14-26. The passage is a long one; I will quote the relevant Scriptures here.

Elihu first asks Job a question.

Why do you complain to him [God]
that he answers none of man's words?
For God does speak—now one way, now another—
though man may not perceive it. (vv. 13-14)

The first way God speaks is through dreams.

In a dream, in a vision of the night,
when deep sleep falls on men
as they slumber in their beds. (v. 15)

Perhaps trying to chide Job slightly, Elihu goes on to say,

He may speak in their ears
and terrify them with warnings. (v. 16)

Had not Job complained that God had terrified *him* through dreams?

When I think my bed will comfort me
and my couch will ease my complaint,
even then you frighten me with dreams
and terrify me with visions. (7:13-14)

Elihu is suggesting something that Job ought to consider now that he is being heard by someone: that those terrifying dreams may be the means by which God is trying to speak to him and win him back, and not to harass him.

Second, Elihu says that God may speak to a person through suffering.

Or a man may be chastened on a bed of pain
with constant distress in his bones,
so that his very being finds food repulsive
and his soul loathes the choicest meal. (33:19-20)

Again, Elihu uses the precise words and concepts of Job's distress, to show not only that he has heard Job but that God has heard him too. "Have you considered," Elihu asks Job, "that God may be doing this for a reason?" What makes Elihu such a remarkable person is that he never, like the other friends, gives a definitive reason for Job's suffering; he does give some plausible suggestions for Job to consider. By doing this he honors Job's integrity to come to a conclusion about his suffering by himself. Suffering, for Elihu, is a mystery through which God tries to communicate with his creatures.

The third way that God may communicate to Job is through a mediator (33:23-26). When Job first mentioned the idea of a mediator or redeemer in Job 19, he was so overcome by the novelty and power of the idea that his heart nearly fainted within him. Elihu shows that he has not only *listened to Job* but also *learned from Job*, because the mediator is now one of the three ways that God may communicate to us! The mediator, according to Elihu, is gracious and spares the suffering one from going down to the pit (Job 33:24).

The spirit of Elihu's conversation with Job is as follows: "Job, have you considered an alternative explanation of your distress? It could be that God is trying to speak with you in some way. I personally know that God does no evil (34:10). So why don't you consider the possibility that God is really *interested* in communicating with you, but that perhaps the blockage in communication is because of *you*, and not because of God? Perhaps, in fact, you are falling prey to the same fault of your friends. You all think that you know how God acts. Maybe, just maybe, you are wrong, or at least you do not have the whole picture of the situation."

Elihu will argue that God's ways are far beyond human comprehension. Several times, as he concludes his long speech, he mentions this:

How great is God—beyond our understanding!

The number of his years is past finding out. (36:26)

Who can understand how he spreads out the clouds,

how he thunders from his pavilion? (36:29)

God's voice thunders in marvelous ways;

he does great things beyond our understanding. (37:5)

It is almost as if Elihu is trying to say, "Job, your world and your God are too small. Broaden your horizons. Lift up your eyes to see the vast expanse of the Creator's majesty."

Elihu Suggests an Interpretation

Though Elihu suggests several possible explanations for Job's distress, he gives his own interpretation of what he really thinks is happening. Elihu is convinced that suffering is the vehicle God uses to speak to people. He says,

> But those who suffer he delivers in their suffering;
>> he speaks to them in their affliction. (36:15)

Note Elihu's words. God speaks to people *in their affliction.* The implication for Job, of course, is that God is trying to speak to him. What, then, is God trying to tell Job? Elihu has an answer for that too.

> He [God] is wooing you from the jaws of distress
>> to a spacious place free from restriction,
>> to the comfort of your table laden with choice food. (36:16)

Each phrase of the verse is suffused with rich biblical cadences. The God who woos Job is the God who woos the harlot Gomer, a symbol of unfaithful Israel, and brings her back to the wilderness to renew her hope (Hosea 2:14-15). God is a "wooer" because God cannot give up his people:

> How can I give you up, Ephraim?
>> How can I hand you over, Israel?
> How can I treat you like Admah?
>> How can I make you like Zeboiim?
> My heart is changed within me;
>> all my compassion is aroused.
> I will not carry out my fierce anger,
>> nor will I turn and devastate Ephraim.
> For I am God, and not man—
>> the Holy One among you.
>> I will not come in wrath. (Hosea 11:8-9)

Elihu is using a word with rich covenantal associations, so that Job will see himself, once again, as the one beloved of God.

The God who will lead Job into a "spacious place" is the God who has led the psalmist into that same broad place.

> The LORD was my support.

He brought me out into a spacious place;

    he rescued me because he delighted in me. (Psalm 18:18-19)

You have not handed me over to the enemy

    but have set my feet in a spacious place. (Psalm 31:8)

The spacious place is a place of freedom, where one has room to stretch, to paint one's life on a broad canvas, to discover and rediscover the fullness of faith and life. Elihu is boldly suggesting that God would do for Job what he does for the psalmist in deepest distress. The spacious place is right around the corner for Job.

I think that today what many of us need is more space. We feel trapped and caught in our lives. Often we take on, or have thrust on us, commitments from which we just cannot seem to extricate ourselves. We need to escape, to breathe again, to draw deep lungfuls of air, to stretch and say, "O Lord, thank you for the broad place!" Elihu's words are a reminder that the "spacious place" is what Job and all of us need, and that to which God is wooing us.

Finally, Job 36:16 speaks of the comfort of the table, laden with choice food. Who can't hear behind this verse the most famous words of that most famous psalm?

You prepare a table before me

    in the presence of my enemies. (Psalm 23:5)

God will prepare a feast for Job, and since God speaks to people amid their distress, perhaps the feast for Job will be right in the midst of his enemies. But who can fear if God the shepherd prepares a feast for us in the middle of our foes? Our cup, indeed, overflows.

Elihu has treated Job like a man and not like a theological argument. He has listened deeply to him, responded sensitively with a variety of explanations, and then answered him biblically with his interpretation of Job's situation. Elihu holds out the olive branch of friendship and the hopeful prospects of a bright future.

Job has not said a word in some time. It is his longest period of silence (six chapters) in the entire book. The silence of Job may be interpreted many ways, but I see it as Job's realization that someone, finally, is speaking *to* and *with* him, and not simply *at* him. Someone has listened and has actually challenged Job to expand his horizons. Job was not expecting this; finally here is one response he cannot find fault with. Job is a man of intellectual honesty and integrity. His silence means that he is beginning to be swayed by Elihu's words to look at his situation in a different way. "Maybe, just maybe, Elihu has something to say. Maybe God is a bigger God than I have anticipated. Maybe I *am* lacking in understanding. Maybe, just maybe, I don't have all the answers." Job is not ready to admit anything yet or even say anything. He still wants to talk to God, but he has been moved.

God Speaks (Job 38—41)

Elihu's arguments have not simply prepared Job's *mind* for God but prepared his *heart* for God. In Job 37, Elihu's last speech, he actually hears a rumbling coming from the north, a rumbling that means that God is coming in person!

At this my heart pounds
 and leaps from its place.
Listen! Listen to the roar of his voice,
 to the rumbling that comes from his mouth.
Out of the north he comes in golden splendor;
 God comes in awesome majesty. (37:1-2, 22)

Elihu's passions are stirred. How could Job's heart be untouched? The big meeting, the meeting for which he has been longing since the beginning of his distress, is finally here! The air is electric. Elihu retreats, and God enters.

God does not introduce himself, or thank Elihu for preparing the way or Job for issuing the invitation. God simply speaks.

God speaks and speaks and speaks. He gives Job a chance to answer him, but Job recoils in unworthiness (40:3-5). Then God just keeps on speaking. At the end Job will respond in a totally unexpected way. He who was once bold, defiant and demanding becomes a broken man. He despises himself and repents in dust and ashes (42:1-6). What is it in God's speech that is able to turn Job around, make him come completely undone and disoriented? What, really, has happened to and in Job?

Two things have occurred in these chapters that are keys to Job's transformation and that become keys to Job's restored trust in God. These two things are Job's glimpse of the majesty of God and his sense of personal disorientation. Both are necessary, I am convinced, to hear and see God in a new way and to trust God again.

God's Majesty

When God speaks in Job 38—41, he doesn't answer Job's questions. Recall that Job had requested an audience with God to "state my case before him and fill my mouth with arguments" (23:4). Job wants God to "fess up," or at least to make known to Job why God is tormenting him so much. Job feels that he has an airtight case. He has done nothing deserving this much punishment and suffering. He has been rehearsing every word for days. Not even God, he thinks, can escape his ironclad logic. Even though God has not spoken to Job directly, Job feels like he has "cornered" God.

So how does God answer Job? He answers Job in his freedom and his majesty. The *tone* and the *content* of God's speech are important to understand. At first God's tone appears to be scathingly sarcastic and maybe even a bit harsh. God says,

Who is this that darkens my counsel
  with words without knowledge?
Brace yourself like a man;
  I will question you,
  and you shall answer me. (38:2-3)

Our first impression is of a God who is rather insulted at Job's forwardness, a bit disturbed at having to justify himself and somewhat eager to show Job how little Job really knows. All of this is present to a degree in God's speeches in Job 38—41.

But the stronger and more dominant tone of the speeches is *invitational*. By showing Job how much he doesn't know about the world, God is not trying to gloat over Job or rub his face in his limitations. Rather, God is, in Elihu's phrase, "wooing you from the jaws of distress to a spacious place free from restriction" (36:16). By revealing who he is to Job, God is inviting Job to enter into a deeper relationship with the God who made and cares for the entire universe. God beckons Job to a different level of knowledge, a more profound sense of intimacy, a deeper acquaintance with nature and God and the order of life. God is "wooing" Job from his rather simplistic theology of retribution, which both he and his friends had adopted, and into the deeper theology of personal relationship. No longer can Job's theology be a series of propositions or belief statements about God; he now encounters the living God, and every human statement to describe God will be incinerated in the heat of God's glorious presence.

The *tone* of God's speech, therefore, is meant to strip Job of all his pretention to knowledge and all his pride at previous accomplishment. It leaves Job naked and quivering. Yet God wounds only to heal, and God unclothes only to further clothe. God invites Job to a deeper level of clothing, to this more profound degree of trust.

The *content* of God's speech takes Job on a tour of the natural world (Job 38) and the animal world (Job 39). God asks Job repeatedly if he has knowledge about the operations of these spheres. He asks if he was present at the "birthing" of the world. Does Job's great knowledge, therefore, come from his age? No response. He asks if he knew how to quell the tumultuous waves of the sea. That is, does Job possess special power? No response. Finally, he asks whether he knows the cycles of nature and the animal world. No response. Job is revealed as ignorant because of his youth, his relative powerlessness and his lack of knowledge of the world. The irony is beginning to dawn on the reader and on Job. Why should a person so ignorant of the majesty and wisdom of God be able to set the rules for the running of the universe?

Of course, God is giving Job this "catechism" bcause he wants to impress on Job the gap between them. Job cannot enter fully into God's world, even though he says he would like to, because God is simply too high and lofty for him. In the words of Isaiah,

"For my thoughts are not your thoughts,
   neither are your ways my ways," declares the LORD.
"As the heavens are higher than the earth,
   so are my ways higher than your ways
   and my thoughts than your thoughts." (Isaiah 55:8-9)

It is dawning on Job that he has requested an audience with the living God and not just with another one of his friends. When pain was his only reality, it was as if his entire world was circumscribed by his own agony. He became the center of his own miserable universe. But now, when he has asked for God, he gets God! And what a God! This God is one who wants to "set the record straight" by showing the tremendous gap between the creature and the Creator.

God is saying to Job that if he wants to talk with him, he will have to enter a new dimension of life. "I am the God who will break all your boundaries and categories. I am the God who exceeds your rigidities and your theologies. You thought you knew me, and that you could 'condemn me to justify yourself' [Job 40:8], but you really don't know me at all. Let me lift you, Job, to a higher plane of thinking, indeed, to the plane of seeing."

Job's Disorientation

It is all too much for Job. He feels his world spinning out of control. He looks up. The heavens whirl. He looks around him. Nothing is still. He looks down. The floor is no longer there. He doesn't know whether he is standing or lying down, whether he is flying or stationary, whether he is safe or in danger. Vertigo. He has lost his moorings and sureness. All his firm knowledge is completely gone. Whatever case he had has been shattered. The prosecuting attorney will now concede the argument, because he just doesn't know anything anymore. Job is undone and disoriented. He is naked before God, like Adam and Eve, but he cannot even muster a feeble excuse. He has no serpent to point to. He, who is already fractured, has been broken into smaller pieces, if that is possible. Listen to Job's words.

Surely I spoke of things I did not understand,
  things too wonderful for me to know. . . .
My ears had heard of you
  but now my eyes have seen you.
Therefore I despise myself
  and repent in dust and ashes. (42:3, 5-6)

In the midst of Job's disorientation comes his great breakthrough. As a matter of fact, confusion and revelation seem to happen at the same time for Job. He sees God (Amen! Hallelujah!) and he despises himself (But why?). Like the prophet Isaiah, who *saw* the Lord high and lifted up, and then uttered, "Woe to me! . . . I am ruined!" (Isaiah 6:5), so Job sees God and despises himself at the same instant. This is a breakthrough, and it will either lead him to the very gates of hell and beyond or into the presence of God.

I will return to this breakthrough in the final chapter to see how it becomes the experience through which Job's life is reoriented and his trust is restored. At this point, however, we must leave Job in the throes of his overpowering vision, covered with dust and ashes. It is not a bad place to leave him, since, for those who suffer, disorientation and confusion is a powerful reality. Let us pray for those who suffer, and for ourselves, that the vision may be the prelude to a new and full symphony of life which God has prepared for us.

Learning from Elihu and God

When Job despised himself and repented (42:6), he must have felt as far from restoration as ever. Yet he wasn't. By this time Job has actually learned three things that prepare the way for his full restoration. These things, when combined with the five lessons from the last chapter, provide practical advice for us on trusting God again.

First, Job learns to listen. It may sound trite or appear unimportant, but this could be the most significant development for Job's restoration. After his great distress all he could do was listen to his own thoughts. The sound of his pain was so deafening that he couldn't hear anything else. Job spoke with his friends for more than twenty chapters, but they really never made contact with each other. The great problems with the Hebrew text of Job 25—27 (Who is speaking? Where does he start and stop?) are an indication to the reader that *no one* knows who is talking. No one, certainly, is listening.

Only with Elihu's speeches does Job begin to listen again, and only because he sees that *Elihu* has heard him. Job recognizes Elihu as someone who is capable of understanding him, and of putting his concern into a broader context. "Someone has heard me. Maybe the world is not simply full of stupid or scared people. Maybe I'm not the only one who is feeling what I do." That is how Job begins to hear again.

The point is powerful for us to consider today. Our ability to trust God again relates to our ability to listen again. My distress sometimes makes me unable to hear the words of another. Believe, friend, that there *is* someone out there who can understand you in your distress and who can put it into perspective. Believe that someone you know may be trying to speak with you, to help you see and hear your distress differently, if you will just listen. Your life and faith restoration may depend on it.

Job also learns that God is a remarkable God, bigger than he ever conceived. We probably all nicely nod our heads to affirm this truth. But, like Job, we need the awareness of his magnificence to absolutely astonish us and ravish our hearts. We might have partial "heart ravishings" when we enter the Chicago Art Institute and see Edward Hopper's 1942 classic *Night Hawks*, or when we behold a Caravaggio painting of John the Baptist in the Nelson-Atkins Museum in Kansas City. But these are only partial experiences when compared with meeting the living God.

To truly learn that God is a remarkable God is something larger than that. It is like a man who has been nearly blind since youth, and who loves impressionist art and has had to study Monet square inch by square inch for fifty years, finally having eye surgery and being able to *see* Monet's water lilies or *Rouen Cathedral* for the first time in their entirety. It is like a deaf woman having a blockage in the inner ear removed and being able to hear the crying of her baby for the first time. It is breathtaking, overwhelming, riveting. It breaks every boundary to understanding that we had feebly erected. It brings forth spontaneous and uncontrollable laughter and tears and great joy. It is new life itself.

Have you ever experienced God in this way? I can suggest no formula that will make it happen. One aspect of God's sovereignty is that he reveals himself when he desires and to whom he desires. But a rereading of Job 38—41 ought to set your heart afire with yearning for the God whose "ways are past finding out."

Finally, Job learns that confusion and trust are not distant cousins but are, in fact, close relatives. Disorientation and clear vision occur for Job at the same time. I will have more to say about this in the final chapter. But if you are confused, disoriented and defeated, take heart. It may mean that your restoration is not far away. Easter Sunday is only two days after Good Friday. If you feel that all you have to give to God is your emptiness, then maybe you are ready to be filled. As a popular Christian chorus says, "All I had to offer him was brokenness and strife, but he made something beautiful of my life." God is still in the business of restoring broken people and in removing the veils of confusion that cover our hearts.

Prayer

Our living God, sometimes I can't help feeling that I contribute to my own distress and lack of trust because I don't listen and because I constantly set limits on you. I have closed my ears, not simply to the insistent cries of hurting people around the world but also to the words of those near at hand. I deny your grace in unexpected places. I draw into my own shell and hear only the noise of my broken heart. Break me out of my self-imposed limitations of hearing and seeing, that I may hear and see you in another way. Give me a sense of your grandeur, O God, and lead me to rest in your greatness. Lead me through the confusion and into the bright hope of an emerging dawn. Through Jesus Christ our Lord, amen.

Questions for Study and Discussion

1. What is your reaction to the story that Tedd told about the Kansas

rancher, his deceased wife and Will?

2. Describe an occasion where you felt someone really listened to you, or when you heard something in a new way. What did this conversation do for you? For the other person?

3. Have you ever had an experience of the awesome majesty or goodness of God? When and where? How did you respond?

4. What do you think Job 42:5 means ("my ears had heard of you but now my eyes have seen you")?

5. What are some things about God and faith that still confuse you? Why do they confuse you? What is your reaction to your own confusion?

JOB 42:16
After this, Job lived a hundred and forty years; he saw his children and their children to the fourth generation.

10

LIVING
DIFFERENTLY
(JOB 42)

Trusting God again after great loss means that we need to think, see and hear differently. We need to be attentive to signs of God's presence and to "little miracles" (to use Julie's words) that he sends our way. The psalmist, confirming my point, says,

Open my eyes that I may see

wonderful things in your law. (Psalm 119:18)

We don't see because we don't look; we don't hear because we don't listen. A large part of trusting God again after great pain is to look and hear differently. Our pain should attune our senses to different things, much as night-vision glasses enable us to see when we thought we were blind.

Yet our restoration is not complete, and our trust is not fully reestablished until we also learn how to *live differently*. We can think and hear and see differently, but until we are able to integrate all these new sights, sounds and thoughts into our daily lives, we still may live in defeat, brokenness and lack of trust. The goal of this chapter is to help you make the choice to live differently, to live in restored trust, to live with the integrity that your life really requires.

Making the Choice

To make the choice. That, truly, is the issue. But our choice to trust God again is not like choosing an entree on the menu or selecting which shade of wallpaper best fits our color scheme. Living differently means that we will live with *different values* and *different expectations.* I will illustrate this by telling briefly what trusting God has meant for me.

I, Glandion, have been a minister for twenty years. For several years I practiced my ministry outside the local congregation, but I have also been a pastor. I think it is accurate to say that I know how to do the "job" of ministry: to preach, teach and administer, to counsel and plan, to speak correctly to and affirm people, to marry, bury and baptize. But I have realized recently how my ministry actually can be hazardous to my spiritual health.

Take a common occurrence in the ministry. I am invited to a women's association lunch and am asked, just before it begins, to say a blessing on the meal. I offer a prayer with no difficulty. By this time in my life the words, *spiritual* words, flow easily from my lips. I return to my office after the lunch, and I start to feel that the prayer was just an act. I reflect further on my ministry and realize that a good portion of my life is me acting in the "role" of the minister. I think of how I am a "religious" man, just as people in my congregation are "medical," "business" or "educational" men and women. We are all competent, polite and capable. We do our work, are paid for it, support each other and have a "successful" career and church.

At that moment I try to pray to God and discover that I can't. The words are not there. The sense of the heart is absent. I realize that when I am on *religious* display I can perform to everyone's expectations, but now when I am alone before God I am speechless. I may be a success as a speaker, a teacher, a citizen, a father, but now I begin to feel empty *as a man.* I listen for God because I know that I don't have anything to say to him.

After a while I feel that God is trying to say something to me, something like the following: "Carney, I know you. I really do. You have put a lot of your confidence in the fact that you have made something out of your life. You play a lot of roles very well. But I'll tell you, what I really want is not you in your roles, but *you*. I will be stripping away your confidence in every human role you play, until you recognize that I am who you say that I am in all your religious pronouncements. Trust me, but things will be different."

I return to myself and feel stripped, naked and empty. I feel my chest and wrist to make sure my vital signs are intact. I feel a tremendous temptation to ignore what just happened, to pick up the phone and return to my "regular" life by turning on my "religious" self to a parishioner. After all, people *are* in need. But this day I do not return to my work. I sit in the chair and begin to talk to God.

To my surprise, I now have no difficulty praying. I say, "God, you know that I am a man in conflict with myself. You know that I want to do well, that my family and I need me to do well, that the people expect me to do well, that our whole economic and religious system is based on the premise that I do well—but O my God, I really am not well. I feel as if I am a fake, a religious counterfeit. I have answers for everyone, but nothing for myself. I really do not know you very well at all, God. And God, I am afraid. I am afraid that if I take my honest concerns to the people, I will either hurt or lose them. I can't go on with this tension, but I don't know if I can go on with honesty alone. Make me into the man you would have me be, and let the role take care of itself."

When I utter the last sentence, I am not sure if I am really saying the truth. I don't know if I really want God to do this for me. I don't have a clear sense of what truth is. All I know is that God *knows* everything about me and that he can do all things. I will have to see how life unfolds after this. I am now living in this time of nakedness, awaiting God's further clothing of me.

I find that Job again is the one I need for my present situation. Job has been my teacher and wise guide, and he will guide me here, too. I believe that Job can be not simply my teacher but *our* teacher because he has learned many different things. He has learned what it means to have life fall apart. He knows loss. He knows the gamut of emotions associated with loss. He has felt anger, confusion, rejection, grief and hopelessness.

He knows what it is not to be understood. He has nearly abandoned any hope for the future.

Yet Job has also discovered that restoration is possible, though it is, for him, a *gradual* process. Job is not like the prodigal son of Jesus' parable, who "came to himself" when he was in the pigsty, rushed home and was immediately greeted by a waiting father and a sumptuous meal. Job is also not like the apostle Paul, who met the risen Christ in his Damascus road vision, a vision which quickly transformed his life. Job's restoration starts quietly when he asks for wisdom (Job 28). Job's personal reformation continues when he learns to think about his past in a new way, when he hears a friend (Elihu) who has first listened to him, and when he is open to the voice of God speaking directly to him.

In Job 42, the subject of this chapter, Job begins to live differently. This "new life" for Job consists of three things: (1) new knowledge, (2) new relationships and (3) new freedom. I emphasize the word *new*, and I will speak about real restoration and renewed trust, because the Scriptures teach that Job's postdistress days were *better* than his earlier days:

> The LORD blessed the latter part of Job's life more than the first.
> (Job 42:12)

That will be my challenge and your challenge now. Can *your* postdistress days be better, richer, more full of grace than your predistress days, those days when, as Job said, "my path was drenched with cream and the rock poured out for me streams of olive oil" (29:6)? Can we dare to hope that grace and satisfaction will attend our remaining days?

A Daring Thought

The basis for our confidence that restoration of trust in God is possible for us, is God himself. God sets the tone for Job's and our healing. In a thought to which I will return below, the text says,

> After the LORD had said these things to Job, he said to Eliphaz the Temanite, "I am angry with you and your two friends, because you have not spoken of me what is right, *as my servant Job has.*" (42:7)

The daring thought is that when all is said and done, after Job's complaints and accusations against God, *God agrees with Job!* Job has spoken correctly about God. He, the one who wished that he had never been born, who called God the attacker, who despaired about life and complained of his agony, *he*, God says, *is correct*. The thought is liberating, because it suggests that those who suffer and speak may be more correct in their speech than those who just speak. It suggests that the Rwandan refugee is a more compelling, eloquent and true spokesperson for the plight of the people than a U.S. State Department official. It teaches that *you*, whose trust has been broken and who have suffered great loss, are a truer speaker about your condition than anyone else, friends included.

Note also that Job's speech *about God* was more true than that of the three friends. Pain, honest feeling and speech from the depths of personal experience reveal truer knowledge about God than the knowledge and speech of professional theologians! The world has been turned upside down. The true speakers about God are those who have spoken with conviction to God and about God out of the depths of their lives.

Job is one such person. Now (in chapter 42) he receives his full restoration. His restoration consists of new knowledge, new relationships and a new future. Let us briefly consider each.

New Knowledge

We left Job in the middle of his overpowering vision, covered with dust and ashes. Job was disoriented by the powerful presence of God. Yet it was in the midst of his confusion that his breakthrough occurred. In the last chapter I described the breakthrough as "seeing differently"; here I will talk about Job's new knowledge, knowledge that sets him on the path of restoration and recovery.

What new thing does Job learn? Let us start with the text of Job 42.

Then Job replied to the LORD:

"I know that you can do all things;

   no plan of yours can be thwarted. . . .

Surely I spoke of things I did not understand,

   things too wonderful for me to know." (vv. 1-3)

Job is overwhelmed because he now *knows* something that he really didn't know before. What is it? He knows now that God can do all things.

It is a most dramatic and powerful statement. *It means that Job has become aware, at the core of his being, and not simply in his system of belief, that God can do all things.*

Job had always *believed* that God was powerful, indeed, that God could do all things. In Job 9, when Job contemplates approaching God with his complaint, he ruminates,

His [God's] wisdom is profound, his power is vast.
    Who has resisted him and come out unscathed? . . .
He speaks to the sun and it does not shine;
    he seals off the light of the stars. . . .
He performs wonders that cannot be fathomed,
    miracles that cannot be counted. . . .
If he snatches away, who can stop him?
    Who can say to him, "What are you doing?" (vv. 4, 7, 10, 12)

One reason Job was ambivalent for so long about approaching God was that he was afraid he would be overwhelmed by this all-powerful God. This makes Job defiant and despairing.

Yet in Job 42:2, when Job confesses that God can do all things, a confession substantially the *same* as in Job 9, everything has changed. Why the change? I believe that in Job 42, Job is now speaking from the level of personal knowledge and not from simple religious belief. He now knows God's power in a way he never has before. But how can that be? What, in fact, does Job mean when he says, "I know that you can do all things"?

I think it means three things for Job and for us. *First, it means that Job finally knows that God was there in his past.* When Job prospered in his earlier days, God was there. When the terrible and sudden events befell him, God was there. When Job cried out in pain and thrashed around in self-pity and anguish and accusation and bitterness, God was there. God was there when Job felt stinging arrows penetrate his flesh.

But God was also there in Job's times of hope. When Job expressed his knowledge that his Redeemer lived, God was there. When Job called on a witness in heaven, God listened. Job has come to believe that God was with him at all times. When he spoke rashly, God heard. When he spoke with eloquence and passion and determination, God heard Job's voice. When Job made miserable mistakes, God heard him also. Job *knows now* as surely as he knows the pain of his body or the fact that his Redeemer lives, that God was there when he went through his trauma.

Such a thought might formerly have increased Job's anger; now it increases his amazement. Formerly he might have bitterly complained, "Well, God, you see everything, and yet you do nothing! You are not worthy to be called my Lord and my God!" Now, when he realizes the scope of God's greatness, Job knows that he is thoroughly known. But he is no longer bitter. He sighs and yearns and is amazed and stupefied. He is sober and wondering at the same time. He is struck by this new knowledge. It is a level of knowing deeper than sexual intimacy, touching the very core of his being. Every fiber and sinew and muscle and bone and tissue is now filled with the awareness that God has always known his plight, better even than Job knew it himself.

Second, Job has learned the holistic nature of knowledge. The word *holistic* is a term that emerges from our own experience, but it can also be applied to Job. When we speak of knowledge today, we speak of it in fragmentary ways. Universities are divided into departments; professorships are in a particular field; specialization of knowledge is the order of the day. In addition, we make the distinction between knowledge of the head and knowledge of the heart, of knowledge "out there" and knowledge "in here," of mastery of a field and mastery of self. Knowledge today is scattered and partial. Few people can supply, and even fewer opportunities in life can provide the "big picture." We live in the details.

But now Job knows something different and something better about knowledge. He knows that *knowledge is one even as God is one*. He has discovered his pain and himself and his God, and he has learned that all are One. In the eloquent final words of Norman Maclean's American classic *A River Runs Through It*, Maclean narrates an experience of finally understanding the oneness of all knowledge:

> In the Arctic half-life of the canyon, all existence fades to a being with
> my soul and the memories and the sounds of the Big Blackfoot River
> and a four-count rhythm and the hope that a fish will rise.
>
> Eventually, all things merge into one, and a river runs through it.

Once again, Job's experience of knowledge puts to shame all our pretensions to knowledge. We in the university who pressure eighteen-year-olds to "declare a major" and specialize, who pride ourselves in the obscurity of our specialized knowledge, who think that the mastery of data will ultimately lead to the mastery of life, are shown by the book of Job to be living in an illusion, a dream world, a self-imposed prison of the soul and mind. Knowledge is a whole, and Job teaches that to us, because he first understood it.

Third, Job has learned, perhaps for the first time, that God is sovereign over all of nature and that God is also completely sovereign over his life. He has learned that God is the sole originating source of energy in the world. All other energy is derivative. God used this energy to make Job. In words dripping with sensuality and delicious in scope, Job declares,

> Did you not pour me out like milk
> and curdle me like cheese,
> clothe me with skin and flesh
> and knit me together with bones and sinews? (10:10-11)

God has also shown his sovereignty in the taming of Behemoth and Leviathan, two ancient monsters who were the scourge of the earth (Job 40—41). The seemingly all-powerful Leviathan is a mere *plaything* to God. God effortlessly controls every power to hurt or destroy. Humans may quake at the power of Leviathan, for "no one is fierce enough to rouse him" (41:10), but God is much greater. In the words of the psalmist, God formed Leviathan "to sport in it" (Psalm 104:25-26 RSV).

What then is there to fear if God is sovereign? What more must we really know if we know that God is sovereign? We might have a tendency to shudder at the threatening terrors of the night, but they are nothing compared to God. With God all things are possible, the Scriptures teach.

Job, finally, to his enduring credit, has not simply believed this, but has *known* it.

Do we believe these things? Do we also *know* that God can do all things? That God has always been there with us, that knowledge is holistic, that God is the sovereign Lord of all? Even the mountain becomes a plain before the Lord (Isaiah 40:4; Zechariah 4:7). Before God the darkness is not darkness anymore, but it is as bright as the day (Psalm 139:12). With God all things are possible. *That* is what brought the breakthrough for Job. Will you let that happen for you?

New Relationships

When Job has his breakthrough experience in Job 42:1-6, he feels conflicting feelings. On the one hand, he knows something that he never really had known before. This new knowledge is *personal, experiential and dramatic.* He knows that God is sovereign over nature, over all the creatures, and over his life too. Job feels that he is known thoroughly, yet he is still loved. He is fully known, yet he is not rejected. God has demonstrated his absolute power to Job, and Job has learned again that his God is also a merciful, wise and saving God. He is grateful and full of God.

On the other hand, Job also feels unworthy. When he "sees God" he is overcome by his inadequacy:

> Therefore I despise myself
> and repent in dust and ashes. (42:6)

The inadequacy Job feels is not because he feels he is worthless, just a piece of garbage. In contrast, Job's inadequacy is expressed better by the question, "Why, O God, should I have doubted you?" or "Who am I that I should have taken so long to discover that you are a wise, powerful and merciful God?" He is amazed and humbled that the Ruler of the universe would do this for him. He feels unworthy, but not worthless. Job knows that he has been more than blessed. Such knowledge is too wonderful for him. It is too good to be true. But it is the sober truth.

These conflicting feelings are resolved by Job's new relationships (42:7-9). Job's relationships with *God and with the three friends* are restored. This restoration teaches us that trusting God again must have a dimension of reconciliation if it is to be genuine. All of Job's relationships were strained to the breaking point. Now they are restored, in ways that no one could have imagined. Let us see how this is true.

Right Relations with God

Take first Job's relationship with God. Job has said some pretty strong statements about God. Remember how Job felt that God had shot his poisoned arrows at him (6:4), gnashed his teeth at him, crushed and shattered him (16:7-14) and alienated people from him (19:13-20). Job felt that even if he resolved to try to "clean up" from the disaster, by washing with snow and cleansing his hands with lye,

> [God] would plunge me into a slime pit
>
> so that even my clothes would detest me. (9:31)

In short, Job accused God of ruining his life for no apparent reason. God is even waiting around to make Job's life more difficult. It is like accusing God of standing around waiting to knock the crutches out from under those who are trying to walk again, then blaming them when they fall down in pain.

How does God respond to Job, when all is said and done? We have already seen God's response, but now we will examine it from the perspective of restored relationships. God answers, in Job 42, by agreeing with Job! In order that we might not miss it, the statement is made twice:

> After the LORD had said these things to Job, he said to Eliphaz the Temanite, "I am angry with you and your two friends, because *you have not spoken of me what is right, as my servant Job has.* So now take seven bulls and seven rams and go to my servant Job and sacrifice a burnt offering for yourselves. My servant Job will pray for you, and I will accept his prayer and not deal with you according to your folly. *You have not spoken of me what is right, as my servant Job has."* (42:7-8)

Let us run through the meaning of this statement carefully. God is rebuking the three for not speak correctly about him. This, in and of itself, is an amazing statement because the friends were the defenders of God.

They were like our modern friends of God who spend their time telling us how God works in the universe and how he works in our life. Job's friends knew the Scriptures, they knew tradition, they knew how God was supposed to work. And they were still wrong. I am scared when God says that the friends were wrong, because I have acted like them on numerous occasions.

God goes on to say that Job has spoken "right" about him. Many scholars suggest this means that the "general tenor" of Job's remarks was correct, or that "God is more pleased with daring honesty than with a superficial attempt to maintain a shallow creed" (David Howard, *How Come, God?* p. 110). While there is some truth to these explanations, it misses the deeper sense of what God is saying.

I believe that God is saying two things here. First, he is commending the *manner* in which Job speaks. Two verses capture Job's manner of speaking to God:

Therefore I will not keep silent;
I will speak out in the anguish of my spirit,
I will complain in the bitterness of my soul. (7:11)
I loathe my very life;
therefore I will give free rein to my complaint
and speak out in the bitterness of my soul. (10:1)

How does Job speak throughout the book of Job? He speaks in the bitterness of his soul. Job finds it impossible to contain himself. He bursts forth in passionate, sarcastic but deeply despairing speech to God. He does not speak the language of humble devotion or unquestioning praise. He will not let propriety restrain or constrain him. His anguish and bitterness are the engines that drive his speech. He is questioning God's intentions for him. This manner is "right" in God's sight. What is right about it is that it flows from the heart *and* the head, from the deepest conscious resources of the individual.

Second, I think that God is saying, "I can take it! I commend not simply the tone in which you said things, but the things themselves." Whether every single sentence of Job was correct is not really the point. Job himself recognizes that his words have been impetuous (6:3), even if they are not words of wickedness or deceit (27:4). He holds out the possibility that he has gone astray (19:4), though he has done nothing deserving the great distress that has come his way.

I envision God as a wonderful foreign-language teacher, who knows that the students will make many mistakes as they learn to speak their new language. The worst thing for such a student is to say nothing. The best thing is to try out the words you know, in various combinations, in hopes that you will make sense. Surely you make mistakes. That is not the point. The point is that your heart and your mouth are seeking to do it right, to find the right phrases to match your desire. Eventually you will learn the language. Job is learning the language of faithfulness as he speaks out of his anguish to God. Learning takes time, and efforts to learn ought to be commended, as God here commends Job.

It is like the conversation of Jesus with the scribe who had just asked him which is the most important commandment. Jesus answered correctly; the scribe commended Jesus in language that showed that he had thought deeply about love of God and neighbor, and Jesus responded, "You are not far from the kingdom of God" (Mark 12:34). Though the scribe may not be all the way there, he is striving and reaching and thinking and speaking for the kingdom. That is commended. *Job* is commended. Job is commended just at the time that he no longer commends himself. He is told that he is right precisely when he doesn't care anymore if he is right. He has God and God has him. In the words of the Song of Songs: "My lover is mine and I am his" (2:16).

A final indication that Job and God are reconciled is that God calls Job "my servant" four times in 42:7-9. Some may not attach great significance to this, but this is double the number of times Job is called that by God in the prologue (Job 1—2). Perhaps this is a hint of the "double blessings" that Job will get in 42:10-17. In any case it is a sign that from God's perspective, Job is in right relationship with him. It is almost as if Psalm 131 were written especially to capture this vivid moment:

My heart is not proud, O LORD,

my eyes are not haughty;
I do not concern myself with great matters
    or things too wonderful for me.
But I have stilled and quieted my soul;
    like a weaned child with its mother,
    like a weaned child is my soul within me. (vv. 1-2)
Satisfaction, peace and service abound. Trust is restored with God.

Right Relations with Friends

Throughout the book it appeared to be God and the friends against Job. The friends acted as if they spoke for God, and Job certainly was alienated from both friends and God. Job was on the margins of life. He lamented plaintively,

But now they mock me,
    men younger than me,
whose fathers I would have disdained
    to put with my sheep dogs. (30:1)

In Job 42:7-9, Job is reintegrated into life. He who was on the margins now moves to the center by becoming reconciled with his friends. Two things happen to them in these three verses.

First, both Job and the friends have to be willing to do something that they were unwilling to do before. The friends need to offer sacrifice for their sins, and Job needs to pray for the friends, so that their sacrifice will be accepted by God. Previously the friends would not have confessed or sacrificed for their sins, for what sin had they committed? They were the pure ones. But they now had to admit their sin.

Job needed to pray for them. How difficult that must have been for him! He, who had referred to them as deceitful people, as miserable comforters, as stupid companions, now had to pray for their wholeness. How could he possibly retain his former opinion of them when he had to pray for their forgiveness? What a wonderful exercise and lesson for us. Reconciliation is built on the solid foundation of prayer for people who have hurt each other.

Second, they each had to perform activities which testified to their own weakness and need of forgiveness. Job was placed in an unusual role for a wisdom teacher—that of a priest. A priest stands between God and the people and offers their gifts to God and God's word to them. By standing in the middle, the priest is able to avert God's judgment from the people and communicate his grace to them.

The author of Hebrews reflects deeply on the role of the priest, and on Jesus' role as our high priest. The priest is "able to deal gently with those who are ignorant and are going astray, since he himself is subject to weakness" (Hebrews 5:2). He knows his weakness, and he is thereby enabled to identify with the people. He knows the grace and call of God, and he thus can intercede to God for them. The priest in the Old Testament is the most important individual who keeps the religious observances going. Job is brought in from the boundaries of life to the center, to a place where he knows his weakness but can truly help others.

The friends also, through their sacrifice, show their weakness and need for forgiveness. The burnt offering, which they had to provide, was one in which the entire sacrifice was consumed in the flames. It was a sacrifice for sins, and by offering it the worshiper was saying, "Lord, I know I am guilty and in need of forgiveness. I offer the whole animal because I dedicate my whole self to you. Take my sin, transfer it to the animal, and receive me as your humble, forgiven servant."

If reconciliation happens between people, it must happen when each is aware of the other's needs and weaknesses. Reconciliation may be happening in the Middle East in our day not because of someone's position of strength, but because the status quo exposes the weaknesses of both parties. Israel cannot endure another ten years of a Palestinian *intifada* (uprising); Palestinians cannot endure another ten years of Israeli occupation. Both feel vulnerable. Both are willing to deal with each other.

So it is in the sphere of personal relationships. I think genuine reconciliation happens in families or friendships because each side recognizes the other as needy and unable to carry on well without them. Reconciliation cannot happen if one side continually refuses to admit that they make mistakes and that they, too, are in need of forgiveness. Reconciliation can occur, however, when we let go of our pretensions to power, wisdom and insight, recognize and admit our frailties and weaknesses, and humbly serve each other. It is too important a gift to be left unopened and unexplored.

Our world and our lives stand in dire and pressing need of reconciliation and new relationships today. As it was two thousand years ago, so it remains today that the peacemakers are blessed (Matthew 5:9). They are blessed because there are so few of them. We are hindered and held back from the promise of reconciliation, peace and new relationships by our unwillingness to trust each other again. New relationships are built on the solid foundation of renewed trust. Won't you signal your willingness to trust people again by praying for those who have hurt you, by sharing in each other's weaknesses and by bringing your relationship back to the loving hands of God? As Job's experience shows, it is never too late to start trusting again.

New Freedom

But trusting God again is not complete until we have discovered the freedom that accompanies restored trust. Freedom is the reason for our salvation (Galatians 5:1):

> It is for freedom that Christ has set us free. Stand firm, then, and do not let yourselves be burdened again by a yoke of slavery.

Freedom is the goal of creation and recreation (Romans 8:21):

> The creation itself will be liberated from its bondage to decay and brought into the glorious freedom of the children of God.

Freedom is the purpose for Christ's ministry on earth (Mark 10:45):

> For even the Son of Man did not come to be served, but to serve, and to give his life as a ransom for many [to set others free].

Job, too, discovers the most exhilarating freedom after his encounter with God. It is both a freedom *from* certain things and a freedom *to do* other things. Together they add up to a new life, a life in which "the LORD blessed the latter part of Job's life more than the first" (Job 42:12).

Job discovers a freedom from religious fear, a freedom from enslavement to possessions and a freedom from anxiety about the future. He is free from all these things because he knows God in a new way. He knows that "no plan of [God's] can be thwarted" (42:2), and so he knows that nothing can come into his life without the permission of his merciful heavenly Father.

It is too much to claim that Job's previous religious life, before his great distress, was motivated by fear, but one verse indicates that fear was an important component of his earlier faith. When Job curses the day of his birth and foresees nothing but trouble, he lets slip a line which tells us much about his predistress religious convictions:

What I feared has come upon me;

what I dreaded has happened to me. (Job 3:25)

This verse shows Job in his honest, but weak, humanity. Even though his predistress religion was blameless and pure, there was an element of fear in his service to God. He sacrificed for his children so that nothing would befall them. He hoped to avert danger by his loyal conduct.

Who could really blame him? Don't we do the same thing? We try to live our lives in a healthy way; we do all that we can to avert danger; we even try to "bargain" with God about life. "If I do such-and-such, God, you will protect my family, won't you?" We fear the worst so that when the second-to-worst happens to us we can say philosophically, "Well, it could have been worse."

Job teaches us that we can be free from these fears. Job was afraid to lose it all, and he lost it all. But he still lived, and if the Bible is to be believed, his latter days were better than his earlier ones. Sometimes in losing it all we realize that the "all" that we lost, that we thought gave meaning in the world, actually gave us more fears than freedom. Job learned the truth that the psalmist points to in Psalm 46:

God is our refuge and strength,

an ever-present help in trouble.

Therefore we will not fear, though the earth give way

and the mountains fall into the heart of the sea. (vv. 1-2)

Once we have taken God as our refuge, once we know that God can do all things, we will not fear what people or nature or circumstances can do to us or those we love. We are ever in God's care.

This freedom therefore takes away Job's anxiety about the future and his enslavement to earthly possessions. Granted, Job "gets it all back" in double measure, but as most readers will recognize this is almost an anticlimax. He "gets it all back" *after* knowledge is gained and trust is restored with the friends. It is only a sign to the reader that Job has learned that the most important lesson is not the possessions but is in knowing God, the giver of every good and perfect gift in life. As Martin Luther wrote so eloquently in "A Mighty Fortress Is Our God,"

Let goods and kindred go, this mortal life also;

The body they may kill; God's truth abideth still.

His kingdom is forever.

What freedom there is in not being possessed by your possessions, in not worrying yourself sick over the innumerable details that no human can control! Open your arms and your heart again to the world, for it has dealt you its worst and you are not destroyed! Fling wide the doors of your heart to the mysteries and blessings of life, for God can do all things, and he grants you mercy and loves you with an everlasting love! Join the wonderful liberty of the children of God.

Finally, Job learns that his freedom is not simply freedom *from* things but is freedom *to do* something. For Job this will mean the possibility of changing Israelite law and custom. Breakthrough on the personal level leads to the most interesting social breakthrough in ancient Israelite history.

The LORD blessed the latter part of Job's life more than the first. . . .
And he also had seven sons and three daughters. The first daughter
he named Jemimah, the second Keziah and the third Keren-Happuch.
Nowhere in all the land were there found women as beautiful as Job's
daughters, and their father granted them an inheritance along with
their brothers. (Job 42:12-15)

The two unique things about this passage are that the *daughters'* rather than the sons' names are given, and that the daughters have an equal share in Job's inheritance. Before this time it was only sons who divided the inheritance. In the special case where there were no sons, the daughters were permitted to get an inheritance, but they were obliged to marry a man from their tribal group (Numbers 27 and 36).

Job, therefore, is probing a new and potentially revolutionary social pattern. We don't hear his reasons for doing this, but I think that once Job has learned that God can do all things and that goods and kindred may simply vanish, he is able to break himself from the way society says he should be attached to them. Society (ancient Israel) said that the sons divide the land, since they continue the name and the life of the family. Job has seen, through personal tragedy, that society's belief can easily become unraveled and reduced to nothing. Therefore, what is so special about society's belief? Why not be free to pursue other arrangements? It might be too much to see Job as a protofeminist, but we can hear, in his willingness to let his daughters inherit on equal terms with his sons, the faintest whisper of what will be shouted by the apostle Paul:

> There is neither Jew nor Greek, slave nor free, male nor female, for you are all one in Christ Jesus. (Galatians 3:28)

Job is a free man because he trusts again. He trusts again because he has learned that God can do all things. He thought he knew that lesson from the beginning, but he did not. Once the waves of distress washed over him, however, he started to learn. He learned what pain is. He learned the anguish and agony of life for the first time. He learned what it means to suffer in loneliness.

But he also learned something very important about *himself* through suffering. He learned that he could not abandon the belief that the universe had meaning, and that there was at the center of existence a gracious, just and powerful presence. At times during his suffering he *wanted* to believe in hopelessness, meaninglessness and emptiness, but he simply could not. Something within him drove him to seek meaning in a Redeemer. But he still had to talk to God. When he finally was in God's presence, hearing his words, it was enough. It was as if his belief in the goodness and power of God now became stitched to his soul. It became etched on his personality more deeply than fingerprints are carved into our flesh. He now *knew*. God could be trusted. Job need not worry.

That, friend, was enough for Job. No wonder he could live. No wonder "he died, old and full of years" (Job 42:17). His eyes had seen the glory of the coming of the Lord. Have your eyes seen? Your wholeness and renewed trust in God will not be far off.

Prayer

Our living God, the source of our life and health forever, break through the walls I construct against you and others, and show me your glory. Give me a sense of your ability to do all things. Make me satisfied with the knowledge that you are God and that you can do all things. Restore my brokenness and my fractured relationships. Help me believe that my latter days may be more blessed than the former days. Send me out in your service, whether it is as a peacemaker or a challenger to society's status quo. Send me, however, knowing that I have been with you, that I know you, and that you are a trustworthy and loving friend. Through Jesus Christ our Lord, amen.

Questions for Study and Discussion

1. What are some things you really know? How do you know that they are true? Why is it important to know what you know?

2. How have you learned these things that you know? Who or what have been your great teachers in life?

3. Have you ever had what you might call a dramatic experience of grace or knowing, like Job had?

4. Jesus called the peacemakers blessed. Where do you see the need for peacemakers or reconcilers today? How might you be a peacemaker?

5. Job's breakthrough led him to leave a share of his goods and property to his daughters, which was not done in ancient Israel. What is the relationship between seeing God and social reform?

6. Do you believe that your latter days will be blessed more than your former days? Why or why not?

CONCLUSION

TRUSTING
DAY BY DAY

We have taken a long journey together with Job. We have seen him, and felt with him, at his best and at his worst. We have seen him in deepest despair, a despair captured powerfully by John Milton in *Paradise Lost:*

Which way shall I fly,
Infinite wrath and infinite despair?
Which way I fly is hell; myself is hell;
And in the lowest deep a lower deep,
Still threatening to devour me, opens wide
To which the hell I suffer seems a heaven. (book 4, lines 73-78)

Yet we have also seen the restored Job, the Job who knew the truth, even several hundred years before Christ, that "if anyone is in Christ, he is a new creation; the old has gone, the new has come!" (2 Corinthians 5:17). We have seen a Job (in Job 42) who could have written with great conviction the opening verses of Psalm 23:

The LORD is my shepherd, I shall not be in want.
 He makes me lie down in green pastures,
he leads me beside quiet waters,
 he restores my soul.

The distance from despair to trusting again is a great psychological and spiritual distance, and many people get lost in the journey. Some never even begin the trip. Of those who have the courage to start, to take the first step on the thousand-mile trip, many may be waylaid by fears, weariness and lack of a sense that the journey really will have a promising end. But for those who follow the route to the end and learn the lessons of Job, there is the promise that their latter days may be full of even more blessings than the former days.

Four Lessons from Job

The first lesson Job has taught us is that *you need to tell the story of your distress*. The goal of this is not to evoke sympathy or to show others how bad your life has become. Rather, the goal is to be able to *see your distress as a part of your whole life's story*. Distress ought to be given its due, but it should not be given more than that. It is a part of your life, not the whole thing. You had a story before the distress, and you will have one after it, and the distress will be an element of that story. I am not saying that your distress is small; I am saying that it is not your whole life. By tying the distress into the course of your life, you will be ready to emerge from the land of deep darkness into the wonderful light of God.

Second, the book of Job teaches us that *trusting God again requires the search for divine wisdom*. We need wisdom because a fully satisfactory explanation for our distress is not available to us solely from human channels. We may seek out counselors and friends; we may have the most tolerant or accepting spouse; but ultimately only we can decide on an explanation for our distress. And to arrive at that explanation, we need wisdom beyond our own and beyond what can be provided by friends. Job 28, the great hymn to wisdom, is an indication that wisdom, *divine* wisdom, was needed to get Job and his friends out of the vicious whirlpool of their thoughts.

When we are in great distress, our minds go round and round at incredible speeds with the same few alternatives before us. We think that we have no choice, that we are enmeshed in the net of circumstances and bad choices, and perhaps even the evil designs of another. We need God's wisdom, God's insight. We need to persevere in prayer with God. We need to believe that God provides, in the words of Andrew Young's spiritual biography, "a way out of no way."

Third, *we must be willing to listen for God's voice, even in unpredictable places.* Job finished speaking in Job 31, and he was no doubt ready to hear God speak to him immediately. Yet God didn't enter until Job 38. In the meantime another person, Elihu, spoke. There would have been several good reasons that Job shouldn't have listened to him. Elihu was young, he was wordy, and he seemed, at first, to be an ally of the friends. What possible wisdom could he bring? But he did bring insight; Elihu's speeches were crucial for Job's recovery of trust.

Tedd and Julie recognized after Will's death that God speaks to us in the most unpredictable ways. *We* are the ones who limit the ways we think that God speaks. Why not be attentive or open to the lessons of nature after a damaging thunderstorm, when the tangled mass of damp, downed branches glistens in the light of a cloudless new day? Why not apply words said by others to others as God's word to us? The spiritual breakthrough for St. Augustine came when he heard the voices of children calling to each other, "Take it and read, take it and read!" They may have been playing a simple game, but he heard their words as the very word of God. So he "took it and read" Romans 13:13, and his life and the Christian church have never been the same. Divine wisdom, like good food, comfortable beds and pleasant hospitality, often comes in out-of-the-way places and from unlikely sources.

Finally, we have learned that *trusting God again requires our rediscovery of the greatness and sovereignty of God.* Our rediscovery of God's greatness often is closely allied to our own feelings of brokenness. We know, with Paul, that "nothing good lives in me, that is, in my sinful nature" (Romans 7:18). Yet this realization, far from distressing us, empowers us. God may wound, but he does so only to heal. God may break, but he does so only to fuse more strongly. God may even appear to kill, but he does so only to make alive.

That, friend, is the glorious good news. God is with us. We are not alone. God can be trusted. Thanks be to God.